"God uses David Ireland to communicat passion and the anointing of the Holy Sp
        —JIM CYMBALA, pasto
                                            author of *Fresh Wind, Fresh Fire*

"David Ireland has achieved what I thought impossible: a primer on cross-cultural relationships that deserves to be heard, heeded, and honored as the primary toccata and fugue of friendship music. You are holding in your hands a genesis gift of stunning originality, creativity, and genius."
        —LEONARD SWEET, PhD, professor, Drew Theological School and
                George Fox University; chief contributor, Sermons.com

"*The Skin You Live In* will help everyone, no matter race or ethnicity, reach a new level of understanding, appreciation, and respect for all people. God's heart concerning diversity is found in this question: 'Why can't it be that way in My House?' This book helps us practically cross racial and ethnic barriers to embrace the cross-cultural life Dr. Ireland envisions across the cultures."
        —FRANCES HESSELBEIN, president and CEO,
                The Frances Hesselbein Leadership Institute

"The struggle and tension within people groups has existed from the beginning of time. The church birthed on the day of Pentecost is described in Acts 2:8-11 as a church of all people. God's statement in Genesis 11:6 attests to the limitless power of all skins working in harmony. In *The Skin You Live In*, Dr. David Ireland takes you on an inner journey of transformation before the outward manifestation. It will challenge you. It will encourage you. It will change you."
        —DR. SAMUEL R. CHAND,
                author of *Cracking Your Church's Culture Code*

"For more than twenty years, David Ireland has been one of the leading thinkers and practitioners in building a multiethnic and multicultural community. He has captured in this book the lessons learned on his remarkable and profoundly significant journey."
        —DR. MAC PIER, president, New York City Leadership Center

"*The Skin You Live In* is a fresh invitation to lifestyles of reconciliation. Dr. Ireland convincingly uses storytelling, scholarship, and Scripture to affirm that we can leave our comfort zones, challenge our barriers, and find places to stand where we can put some real skin in the game of reconciliation, the way Christ did through His incarnation. Read this practical book!"

—RUSSELL W. WEST, PhD, associate dean, Beeson International Center; professor, Intercultural Leadership Education

"David Ireland is a leader fiercely committed to championing unity and healthy relationships across racial lines. Compassionate and caring, his Christian witness goes far beyond words. In an hour when racial rhetoric and coded messages once again seem acceptable, we need his voice. This book should be required reading for all who are serious about understanding those who 'don't look like us' yet bleed like us! We are one."

—BISHOP DONALD HILLIARD JR., senior pastor, Cathedral International, Perth Amboy, New Jersey; presiding prelate, Covenant Ecumenical Fellowship and Cathedral Assemblies

"With the depth of wisdom you'd expect from a pastor of more than twenty-five years, David Ireland shares a wealth of insight on the pressing issue of race relations within America. Where the book shines brightest is in its blueprint for bridging the racial divide. If you are a Christian, the bridge building is your responsibility, and Dr. Ireland shows you how to go about it. This book is exactly what twenty-first-century people need."

—MICHAEL G. SCALES, EdD, president, Nyack College and Alliance Theological Seminary

"Dr. Ireland is a leader who truly embodies the messages he trumpets. *The Skin You Live In* is an important call to unity as well as a practical how-to manual on achieving it. I recommend this vital message in hopes that we as a body move into genuine, biblical friendships that transcend every area of divide."

—REV. DR. ROBERT STEARNS, author of *No, We Can't: Radical Islam, Militant Secularism and the Myth of Coexistence*

THE SKIN YOU LIVE IN

Building Friendships Across Cultural Lines

DAVID D. IRELAND, PHD

NAVPRESS

Discipleship Inside Out®

NAVPRESS
Discipleship Inside Out®

NavPress is the publishing ministry of The Navigators, an international Christian organization and leader in personal spiritual development. NavPress is committed to helping people grow spiritually and enjoy lives of meaning and hope through personal and group resources that are biblically rooted, culturally relevant, and highly practical.

For a free catalog go to www.NavPress.com
or call 1.800.366.7788 in the United States or 1.800.839.4769 in Canada.

ISBN-13: 978-1-61291-096-3

Cover design by Arvid Wallen
Cover image by cupoftea/Shutterstock

Some of the anecdotal illustrations in this book are true to life and are included with the permission of the persons involved. All other illustrations are composites of real situations, and any resemblance to people living or dead is coincidental.

All Scripture quotations in this publication are taken from the *Holy Bible, New International Version*® (NIV®). Copyright © 1973, 1978, 1984 by Biblica, used by permission of Zondervan. All rights reserved.

Ireland, David, 1961-
  The skin you live in : building friendships across cultural lines / David D. Ireland.
    p. cm.
  Includes bibliographical references.
  ISBN 978-1-61291-096-3
  1. Christianity—United States. 2. Interpersonal relations—Religious aspects—Christianity. 3. Church and minorities—United States. 4. Race relations—Religious aspects—Christianity. 5. Ethnic relations—Religious aspects—Christianity. 6. United States—Race relations. 7. United States—Ethnic relations. I. Title.
  BR515.I74 2012
  261.0973—dc23

                          2012012956

Printed in the United States of America

1 2 3 4 5 6 7 8 / 17 16 15 14 13 12

To my children,
Danielle and Jessica Ireland

ALSO BY DAVID D. IRELAND

Activating the Gifts of the Holy Spirit

Journey to the Mountain of God

Perfecting Your Purpose

Secrets of a Satisfying Life

Why Drown When You Can Walk on Water?

CONTENTS

INTRODUCTION

My wife, Marlinda, was expecting our first child, and her taste buds were all over the place. One night, I headed to the supermarket with one goal: to pick up everything she craved. As a twenty-five-year-old husband, soon-to-be father, newly employed environmental engineer, and pastor of a two-week-old congregation of eight people, I felt a bit inadequate. But I was willing to tackle every one of my new challenges.

As I walked through the electronic doors and started loading up my basket, the thought of encountering God in that supermarket was the furthest thing from my mind. I couldn't have imagined I would have an encounter that would set me on a lifelong trajectory of emotions, research, and spiritual passion during such a mundane errand.

Just as I was placing a jar of pickles into my basket, I noticed Caucasians, African-Americans, Latinos, Asians, and Native Americans at the other end of the aisle all shopping for their weekly groceries. While I stared, captivated by this snapshot of diversity, the Holy Spirit spoke to me, asking, "Why can't it be like that in My house?" Suddenly a whirlwind of emotions churned inside of me. Right there, in the middle of the supermarket, I began to cry uncontrollably. Embarrassment was the last thing on my mind. At that moment, God had touched me with His feelings about racial diversity and His church. Tears were still rolling down my face when I reached the cashier, who probably thought I was trying to scam her for some free food. I was still an emotional wreck after handing her the money and walking out of the store with my bags.

That day I received more than groceries at the supermarket; I received a vision for my life. God's house was meant to be racially and culturally diverse. I had profoundly discovered it as the cry of His heart, and He had shared it with me in a personal way. I suddenly wanted to answer His question—"Why can't it be like that in My house?"—in every way that I connected with other people. The question gnawed at my heart, expanding from ideas about the church to hopes and dreams for society. Soon the question became profoundly personal and I asked myself, *Why can't it be like that in my world?* That meant that everything in my world had to change and I had to make my personal, professional, and pastoral life reflect what God shared with me in that supermarket. Each of my personal relationships had to be examined and scrubbed to see if they measured up to my newfound value for living a multicultural lifestyle.

WHY I WROTE THIS BOOK

Personal relationships are the bedrock to all aspects of social life. They are also the gateway to the corporate boardroom, the police force, and every place of influence in all sectors of society. Hence, if you can learn how to develop cross-race friendships on a personal level, the principles can be applied to the other arms of your life, be they professional or social. The personal relationship is the laboratory where we research and learn how to get along with others.

The New York Times confirms my observation, reporting that whites have been a minority in New York City since the 1980s; the 2010 census shows that trend has expanded to the surrounding region, including northern New Jersey—my home. This identical trend is also occurring across the United States. Although 49.6 percent of greater New York City is white, a persistent racial and gender gap still exists in executive and managerial positions. Interestingly enough, this gap is becoming narrower for white women.[1] The reason: White men—the demographic that largely occupies the boardroom and other places of decision making—have personal relationships with their sisters, mothers, and daughters. They understand how to relate to white women because they are already relationally experienced in this area, so the idea of including them in upper levels of management is a natural progression.

If white males had healthy personal relationships with Asians, African-Americans, and Hispanics, diversity would be easier to achieve in the workforce, communities, the church, and other arenas of life. Equally important is the converse of this statement: If Asians, African-Americans, and Hispanics learned how to cultivate and enjoy personal relationships with members of the white community, the racial gap would become narrower. It's a long-standing social fact that isolation anchors attitudes of prejudice toward other cultures and races.[2]

Because prejudice is everyone's problem, reconciliation must become everyone's responsibility.

Diversity management cannot be legislated by laws, quota systems, or even well-thought-out campaigns by corporate diversity officers. Racial diversity and inclusion begins in the heart and becomes evident in one's personal lifestyle. That is where I had to begin. *My* heart had to change, and *my* lifestyle had to confirm the change.

Shortly after I arrived home with the groceries and shared my experience with Marlinda, I spent most of that evening on my knees before God. From the depth of my soul, amid sobs and tears, came words of promise and obedience. She joined me in adopting this new worldview. We vowed to make it our lifestyle to follow Christ across the cultural divide. We realized that we would have to live counterculturally even within the Christian community. Because only 3 percent of churches in our nation have at least 11 percent of the congregation stemming from a different race than the majority, our churches are still largely monoracial; 79 percent of the Christian church still gathers on Sunday mornings by race.[3] And because personal relationships affect church growth, these statistics presumably also reflect the cross-cultural practices of individuals.[4] Some may not see the need to appreciate diversity as a problem that demands our personal commitment to remedy, but Jesus does.

Having had our first African-American president, it's easy for some pundits to dub this era as "post-racial" America. But our country's present racial realities suggest otherwise. Just take a look at some of the media headlines or the regularity that public apologies are demanded from some celebrity or political leader who spews racial slurs in the heat of anger.

Although it's clearly premature to label these contemporary times "post-racial," we cannot lose sight of the goal to develop healthy cross-race relationships. We can only hope that our children and grandchildren experience life in a post-racial America where race will not be an issue. Certainly, the enemy called *prejudice* has been dealt strong blows over the past several decades through civil-rights legislation, equal-employment laws, the rise of the interracial church, emphasis on political correctness, and more. But giving people the desire to form healthy cross-race relationships is still wanting.

In the words of Thomas Paine, one of America's Founding Fathers, "These are the times that try men's souls." And I piggyback on that statement by saying that these times require our complete obedience to answer Christ's call to cross cultures and love people. Remember, Jesus didn't teach easy discipleship! Neither should we. To become bona fide disciples of Jesus Christ, we can't simply *know* about the doctrine of reconciliation; we must *practice* it.

Reconciliation is a word that captures the social interaction of two people or groups formerly at odds with one another. We recognize that reconciliation has occurred because the issue is settled and the people or groups previously at odds are now at peace with each other. This peace is shown by their ability to get together socially, whether over a meal, in worship, or in another social venue. Paul explained this when he wrote, "If anyone is in Christ, he is a new creation; the old has gone, the new has come! All this is from God, who reconciled us to himself through Christ and gave us the ministry of reconciliation" (2 Corinthians 5:17-18).

The greatest example of reconciliation is when God chose to establish peace with sinful human beings through the sacrificial death of His Son, Jesus. Christ's atoning death reversed our former state of social alienation and disconnection from God. We have been reconciled to God. Reconciliation unites. Reconciliation is a sign of a healed relationship. Likewise, if we are reconciled to other races, our relationships must demonstrate the fact that the alienation has been healed. One inescapable proof of a healed relationship is that peaceful social interactions can and do occur.

How does one become an authentic reconciler—a person who naturally forms cross-race relationships? This is the crux of the book, and I will answer this question by drawing from three areas of my life.

First, I answer this question with findings from my doctoral dissertation, titled "Minority Perspectives of Interracial Relationships in Large Multiracial Churches."[5] As part of my research, I examined eight multiracial churches across America. My thinking was that if a congregation had 40 percent Caucasian members, 30 percent African Americans, 20 percent Latinos, and 10 percent Asians and other, something special had to be going on there. I wanted to uncover what that "something special" was. What were the reasons behind the formation and maintenance of healthy cross-race friendships within the church? I believe that these same principles can be applied to forming friendships across racial barriers within the other communal areas of your life (work, school, and so on).

Second, for the past twenty-five years, I have pastored a multiracial megachurch that my wife and I planted in 1986. Christ Church is a multisite church that represents more than forty different nationalities. I've learned many lessons from my failures and successes in challenging people to embrace God's call to live beyond the safety of their own cultural walls.

Third, I spent time over the past several years functioning as a cross-cultural coach to the National Basketball Association. My task was to help the more than eighty rookies who enter the league each year become more attuned to race and cross-cultural issues. This consulting opportunity arose because basketball is now an international sport. Effectively assimilating international players into the NBA has become a priority because it has both economic and relational implications.

I've helped many people develop strong cross-race friendships, and my hope is that this book will motivate and equip you to do the same. Becoming comfortable in cross-cultural settings and interactions will enable you to help others work through their strained cross-cultural encounters. I want to teach you what I have learned in answering the question the Lord put to me in the supermarket: "Why can't it be like that in My house?"

THIS BOOK'S PROMISE

Quite a number of books on the market decry the ills of prejudice and give the plea for reconciliation, but few tell us *how* to build cross-race relationships. This book is for you if you desire to reach beyond your cultural walls into someone else's life. It will help you answer the following questions:

- Am I cross-racially attractive?
- Do I unconsciously reject people of other cultures?
- How do I develop strong interracial relationships?
- What skills are needed to have a safe interracial conversation on race?
- How can I lead a multicultural team?

- What does a healthy interracial friendship look like?
- How can I help others embrace diversity as passionately as I do?

I have also written a companion six-lesson study guide to help you apply what you learn from this book about developing cross-race friendships. You can access this study guide at www.navpress.com/theskinyoulivein.

Bridging the racial divide between you and those who are different from you offers untold benefits. But before you can help others form healthy cross-race friendships or get through the pain of prejudice, you must become fully exposed to God's love for people, His multicolored people. You must live according to Jesus' value system: "Love your neighbor as yourself" (Luke 10:27). This command extends to matters involved with loving and living with your neighbors.

It will also help you fulfill the Great Commission, which is in peril of being ignored or mishandled. Jesus' command to "go and make disciples of all nations" (Matthew 28:19) cannot be carried out if you lack the skills and willingness to connect cross-racially. This command assumes that we are comfortable and effective in connecting across cultural and ethnic lines. It also assumes that Christians have Jesus' cross-cultural DNA, regardless of how well or how poorly we may be faring in that role right now. The skill can be brought out of its latent state because our Master is the consummate reconciler and His followers have been born into His bloodline.

The following story illustrates how our own personal commitment to developing cross-race relationships is valuable both to us and to members of other cultures. To complete his dissertation, a graduate student was required to live with a

Navajo family for several months. The matriarch of the family, a wise old grandmother, spoke no English, and this doctoral student spoke no Navajo. Yet a bond began to be forged between them, partly with the help of the old woman's children, who spoke English. The student and the grandmother grew to be very close.

Several months later, when the graduate student had gathered all of his data, it was time for him to return to the university. The members of the Navajo village threw a farewell party for him. After the party, as he was getting ready to get into his car, the grandmother hurriedly walked out of the house, tears streaming down her cheeks. She came right up to the student (the first white friend she'd had in her eighty-two years of life), tenderly placed one hand on the left side of his face and the other hand softly on his right cheek, looked him square in the eyes, and said in the best English she could muster, "I like me best when I'm with you."

At that, the young man lost it. He and the grandmother wept together because they had personally experienced how crossing cultures brings out the best in you. When we remain in our own cultural world, parts of us—good parts, lovely parts, culturally important parts—lie dormant. Consider *The Skin You Live In* a safe place where you can let down your guard and receive cross-cultural coaching from a follower of Jesus Christ. My prayer is that you will one day be able to say, *I like me best when I'm with you.*

CHAPTER 1

LEAVING YOUR COMFORT ZONE

I can be a coward in some areas but adventuresome and insanely daring in others. One bright afternoon, I thought, *Why not compete in a triathlon?* You know, that sport that includes swimming in open waters, biking, and running—all in a row. The reason the idea was so far-fetched, at least to my wife, was because I was forty-six years old and had never learned to swim. Because I had competed in a few half marathons and an entire marathon, I knew the running part would be easy. The biking portion would be a challenge because the last time I rode a bike was as a teenager. Competing in the swimming portion bordered on ridiculous.

But my mind was made up. I was going to venture into the open waters only to gain the personal bragging rights of having finished a triathlon. I set a date of one year to accomplish this feat. My first step was to take swimming lessons. I put on my best game face and drove to the local YMCA for swimming lessons. Even after the first two months, I could barely walk ten feet in the shallow end of the pool. It just wasn't working.

I bought a few books on the art of swimming and returned to the pool more determined than ever that I was going to learn how to swim, even if it killed me. I improved slightly. I used every fin and floater my instructor gave me to make it from one end of the pool to the other.

After a few more months, I was able to shed those accessories and reach the other end of the pool. Once there, I hung on for dear life, gasping to catch my breath. After my instructor coaxed me out of my comfort zone — the pool wall I was hanging onto — I made it back to the shallow end of the pool, where I was able to stand up. Each week I returned to the pool simply because I had vowed that I would compete in a triathlon.

To accelerate my learning, I registered for a weeklong swim clinic for beginners to the world of triathlons. Three times a day, we had to go into the Atlantic Ocean off the shore of the island of St. John to learn to swim in open waters. About a month before the race, I finally learned how to swim, float on my back, and move in the right direction in open waters without losing my navigational bearings. When race day finally came, I stood in front of the Long Island Sound wearing my wet suit with hundreds of other triathletes waiting for the signal to plunge into the freezing salt water. As soon as the gun went off, I raced to meet my fears. There I was, swimming in the open waters fed by the Atlantic Ocean. After thirty-four minutes or so, I staggered out of the Long Island Sound, one mile from the place where I entered. To my surprise, I had done it. The rest, though equally difficult — twenty-five miles of biking followed by about six miles of running — was going to be on land. *Praise God*, I thought. *Land sounds good. I'll finish this race. I may not take first place, but I will finish.* And finish I did. They gave me my medal, proof that I had ventured out of my comfort zone and accomplished the task.

This experience taught me three lessons about comfort zones that can be applied to the world of diversity:

1. Comfort zones restrict your view.
2. Comfort zones limit your growth.
3. Leaving your comfort zone forces you to change.

1. COMFORT ZONES RESTRICT YOUR VIEW.

When it came to swimming, my comfort zone had a mental hold on me. The thought of learning to swim, especially in open waters, was unnerving. All kinds of mental images flashed before me, and they all had the same ending: *You can't swim! You shouldn't even try to learn how to swim. The idea of swimming in open water is preposterous! Give it up!* The thought of leaving the safe borders of my comfort zone was terrifying. Something similar happens to many of us when we envision living beyond the safety of our cultural walls. The thought creates fear that is designed to validate our non-cross-cultural choices.

This was the case with Peter when God tried to woo him beyond the safety of his Jewish culture into the world of multiculturalism, where multiple cultures peacefully coexist. As the account goes:

> About noon the following day as they were on their journey and approaching the city, Peter went up on the roof to pray. He became hungry and wanted something to eat, and while the meal was being prepared, he fell into a trance. He saw

heaven opened and something like a large sheet being let down to earth by its four corners. It contained all kinds of four-footed animals, as well as reptiles of the earth and birds of the air. Then a voice told him, "Get up, Peter. Kill and eat."

"Surely not, Lord!" Peter replied. "I have never eaten anything impure or unclean."

The voice spoke to him a second time, "Do not call anything impure that God has made clean."

This happened three times, and immediately the sheet was taken back to heaven.

While Peter was wondering about the meaning of the vision, the men sent by Cornelius found out where Simon's house was and stopped at the gate. They called out, asking if Simon who was known as Peter was staying there.

While Peter was still thinking about the vision, the Spirit said to him, "Simon, three men are looking for you. So get up and go downstairs. Do not hesitate to go with them, for I have sent them." (Acts 10:9-20)

Peter's vision was not about food per se, but God was using the four-footed animals and reptiles as symbols of how Peter viewed the Gentiles. He saw them as impure and unclean people undeserving of God's forgiveness and cleansing through faith in Jesus Christ. In fact, the comfort zone of Peter's culture had created a huge blind spot in how he saw people who lived outside of his culture. Peter realized that his perspective, which was also a symptom of prejudice, was wrong the moment he set foot in Cornelius's house:

Talking with [Cornelius], Peter went inside and found a large gathering of people. He said to them: "You are well aware that it is against our law for a Jew to associate with a Gentile or visit him. But God has shown me that I should not call any man impure or unclean." (Acts 10:27-28)

The comfort of his culture had limited Peter's personal and social experiences with Gentiles. Like any other first-century Jew, Peter dealt with members of the Gentile world in the marketplace, courthouse, and other places of commerce. But he lacked experience that was social and personal — experience that could lead to the expansion of his perspective and appreciation of diversity. Peter obviously found his culture safe and secure and the Gentile's culture potentially harmful, unimportant, and without value. His comfort zone caused him to unconsciously develop a restricted and negative view of the Gentiles, much like our comfort zone confines us to the social borders of our own culture and race.

2. COMFORT ZONES LIMIT YOUR GROWTH.

One Chinese proverb says, "If you don't step out of your comfort zone and face your fears, the number of situations that make you uncomfortable will keep growing." Fear of leaving my comfort zone seriously jeopardized my aspirations to be a swimmer — a triathlete swimmer, no less. Had I not ventured out into the waters, literally, I would not have learned to swim.

Similarly, because Peter had developed relationships exclusively with members of his own culture, his growth as both a person and an apostle was limited. Had Peter ignored or disobeyed the promptings of the Holy Spirit, he would have become a prisoner to his own culture. The opportunity to learn that he ought not to "call anything impure that God has made clean" (Acts 10:15) came when his cultural comfort zone was shattered by the vision. Peter was so entrenched in his cultural perspective that God had to present the vision three different times to help him consider that there was life beyond his culture.

Leaving your comfort zone is no small feat; it calls for you to take a risk. But if you don't venture beyond your comfort zone, your personal growth is at stake. If Peter hadn't embraced the vision, Cornelius and the other Gentiles would not have had the opportunity to receive Christ as their Savior, at least not through Peter's ministry. Peter grew as he became an eyewitness to the workings of the Holy Spirit in other cultures. He grew because he ventured into the home—the personal and social space—of a Gentile. He saw with his own eyes how they lived, ate, and interacted among themselves.

Peter also learned that Cornelius did not hold the same view toward Jewish people that the apostle held toward Gentiles. Cornelius did not consider Jews impure or unclean. In fact, Scripture points out that he fell at Peter's feet in reverence (see Acts 10:25). Cornelius was honoring Peter despite the difference in their cultures. Peter, on the other hand, had to work through his cross-cultural issues. He didn't question whether there were decent and God-fearing Gentiles. He knew that from walking with Jesus. Peter was there when Jesus healed the centurion's servant of a life-threatening illness. The Jews said this centurion—a Gentile—"loves our nation and has built our synagogue" (Luke 7:5). But I suspect that Peter's thinking, even moments before venturing into Cornelius's home, was, *Just because a Gentile is a good person does not mean I can or should befriend him.*

Many people equate professional behavior toward people of other cultures with reconciliation. It's not the same! Reconciliation requires personal association with another person. It's not enough to simply have good thoughts about people or even to merely show them respect. You have to venture into their social world as if Jesus' command to "love your neighbor as yourself" (Luke 10:27) really matters to you. This was exactly what the Holy Spirit was challenging Peter to do. He had to enter the personal world of Cornelius. Peter could not maintain a comfortable distance and wish the best for Cornelius and his group. Cross-cultural growth demanded that Peter go beyond the walls of his own culture.

My friend Bob always talks about his burden to reach Muslims for Christ. When he moved some two hours from where he used to live, one of the first things he did was visit the neighborhood mosque. Talk about being brave. Bob was brave. Not only is Bob a strong Christian who is on fire for the Lord but he's white. In fact, he's on the paler side of white.

Despite the color of his skin, Bob has lots of Middle Eastern friends, and their relationship is not stilted by a religious overture that says, "Let's get to know one another as Christians and Muslims." No, Bob has genuine friendships with black Muslims, Persian Muslims, and Muslims of every other shade and type. His passion to see Muslims won for Christ breaks down cultural walls, shatters empty professional relational associations, and gives Bob access into their homes and lives as a real friend. Bob told me, "I feel like I have a personal responsibility to help unreached people get access to the gospel. I've asked God to use me, and my heart became full of passion and love for the Muslim people."

By the way, when Bob walked into that mosque, he struck up a conversation with the imam and other men curious as to why this pale-looking white guy was interested in talking about Islam. Once again, Bob began making new friendships across racial, cultural, and religious lines. Bob doesn't have a comfort zone, at least not with Muslims. His starting point in becoming a reconciler occurred when he decided that

reconciliation was his responsibility and not just the anony-
mous and invisible *everybody's* responsibility.

3. LEAVING YOUR COMFORT ZONE FORCES YOU TO CHANGE.

The third time the Holy Spirit sent Peter the vision of four-
footed animals, it was becoming very uncomfortable for him to
stay within his cultural comfort zone. He had a major decision
to make: He could either remain a monocultural man, which
would be an act of disobedience to God's call for him to connect
with Cornelius (see Acts 10:20), or he could break out of his
comfort zone into the world of cross-cultural discipleship. Peter's
personal value toward obedience to God became his passport
into the land of diversity. It wasn't easy, but he obediently followed Christ outside of his culture. God calls us to do the same.

Breaking out of your cultural comfort zone requires that
you become a true reconciler. A reconciler is one who believes
in the doctrine of reconciliation and incorporates the habit of
building cross-race friendships as an important value in his or
her lifestyle. A reconciler is one who does not have to be forced
to develop healthy cross-race friendships. The term *reconciler*
is used to describe one who easily forms and maintains cross-
race relationships. Authentic reconcilers:

1. Are at peace with people of other races
2. Know how to build bridges to other cultures
3. Value people of different races living in community

1. Be at peace with people of other races.

Ruthie, a white American friend of mine, is a single parent
by choice. When she adopted an African-American baby boy,

she wasn't prepared for the sideways glances and scrutinizing stares she and her son would receive almost daily. "The looks range from curiosity, sort of 'Hmmm, that's odd,' to outright indignation and disapproval, like 'How could you?'" Ruthie said. "It makes me so angry; I could just strangle these ignorant people!"

Recently, Ruthie and her son, Jack, now seven years old, boarded an airplane. She was warmly greeted by a flight attendant who, like Ruthie, was an attractive blonde-haired, blue-eyed woman. The flight attendant, who was serving Ruthie's section of the plane, was very accommodating, until she heard Jack call Ruthie "Mom." That's when the flight attendant's friendly smile took a distinctive turn. Clearly uncomfortable with the unlikely pair, she subtly but insistently tried to persuade Ruthie to give up to a white couple the choice seats she had selected for herself and Jack.

Ruthie stood her ground, demanding that she and Jack stay put. She won. The flight attendant moved to another section of the airplane, but her inability to interact even on a professional level with interracially paired passengers made her culturally insensitive and unattractive.

Unlike this flight attendant, authentic reconcilers choose to embrace a lifestyle of peace with other races. They hold no hostility toward other ethnic groups.

After all, can you build a healthy relationship with people of other cultures when you're constantly on guard? I don't know of any relationship that can survive a nonverbal but clear attitude that says, "I'm watching you out of the corner of my eye to make sure you always treat me right, racially. And if you don't, I'll put you in your place in a split second!"

If you find yourself becoming uncomfortable or irritated around people who are racially different from you, perhaps you need to spend time analyzing this area of your life. Just as your blood pressure is a measurement of your medical health, the disturbance of your sense of peace is a measurement of your emotional health. It should not be ignored. Don't dismiss the value of walking in peace toward members of other races.

In the Bible, the apostle Paul wrote that true love — the humanitarian kind of love — is "not easily angered [and] keeps no record of wrongs" (1 Corinthians 13:5). It is also true that false love is easily angered and keeps all records of wrongs. No one can live under the pressure a hypersensitive life creates. Real love and peace toward others is achieved only when you keep no record of wrongs they've committed.

I am not suggesting that people should be allowed to get away with racial injustices. They should be penalized appropriately if found guilty of wrongdoing. But authentic reconcilers have peace in their hearts toward members of other races. This peace is evidenced in their demeanor and in the way they express themselves in racially unpleasant moments. They don't feel the need to police others in their cross-cultural interchanges. Their attitude says, "I'm at peace with you and members of other races."

Can you imagine the awkwardness and tangible disconnect you would experience if you held the people in your life personally responsible for all the wrongs their race committed against your race throughout history? It would be impossible for you to live your life to its fullest while lugging around this burden. By acknowledging that every human heart harbors the potential to harm others — those who look like you as well as those who look different from you — you will be at peace with other races. Understanding that we all have the same potential to do evil can keep you from blaming others for the injustices caused by members of their ethnic group.

But being a reconciler requires more than holding to a perspective that sets peaceful coexistence as the goal to achieve. In the same way it took more than one swim in the ocean for me to qualify as a triathlete, it takes more than one visit to a Gentile's home or one missions trip abroad for a person to qualify as a reconciler. Cross-race relationships won't form unless you build bridges across cultural lines through regular expressions of love, compassion, and acceptance.

2. Know how to build bridges across cultural lines.

At a fund-raiser I attended recently with my daughter Danielle, a guy whom I'll call Henry greeted us warmly. He was a middle-aged, jolly white guy who would turn every stranger into a friend in short order. It looked as though Danielle and I were to be next on his list of new friends.

After a few pleasantries, Henry whipped out his wallet, featuring family photos. He was a proud husband, father, and grandfather. He told us that he and his wife of thirty-two years had never had children of their own, so they had become foster and adoptive parents. What was unique about Henry's family photo was that it resembled a general session at the United Nations. Talk about diversity. The world's races were fully represented. Henry's words, friendly attitude, and multiracial family demonstrated that he was a reconciler and knew how to build bridges across cultural lines.

I asked Henry a few questions, beginning with, *What made you decide to adopt kids of different races?* Henry eagerly answered as if he'd been asked this question many times over the years. "My parents were very prejudiced against everybody. You name it, they hated it. So when I became an adult, married, and discovered we could not have children of our own, my wife and I decided that if the world was going to change people like my parents, it would start with us. We took on the fight against bigotry by becoming cross-cultural even when it wasn't fashionable some thirty years ago," he said. "And our love for people evolved into opening our homes and hearts to children in need." Henry saw reconciliation as a personal responsibility and consequently built a bridge of love to other cultures.

To be a reconciler does not mean you have to take in racially diverse foster children, lead public marches holding up "We are the world"-type placards, or become a spokesperson of multiculturalism. Some may choose those paths, but people who choose to quietly effect change within their own social circles can be just as impactful. When you are in the business of connecting with people across racial and ethnic lines, you are a cross-cultural ambassador, a reconciler. Being at peace with others is a core value that flows out of your life. You build bridges by modeling diversity, not by just giving verbal assent to it.

When you model diversity, others around you will learn *how* diversity is to be lived out in a way that is genuine, open, and honest in light of the thorny problems that often arise in race relations. Modeling diversity allows the power of influence to take effect. Your actions will empower others to develop a cross-racial appeal in their own personal and professional lives.

Reconcilers go beyond the point of peaceful coexistence and build bridges by embracing diversity as a lifestyle value they openly defend, if needed. The groundbreaking work by famed behavioral scientist Milton Rokeach on human values provides a wonderful working definition for *values*. Values are "interests, pleasures, likes, preferences, duties, moral obligations, desires, wants" of human beings.[1] They are directional; they affect our preferences and behavior in social ways. For that reason, reconcilers are in the habit of building bridges across the cultural divide based on such things as interests, preferences, and duties rather than forming relationships solely based on race. They love their neighbors as themselves and want to connect socially with them.

3. Value people of different races living in community.

Remember Rodney King's now infamous cry for unity, "Can't we all get along?" King was desperately trying to add his voice to the rallying cry of many to stop the 1992 riot in Los Angeles. This African-American man had been the victim of police brutality at the hands of four white Los Angeles policemen in March 1991. When the officers were acquitted, the verdict set off six days of fiery and violent unrest. Looting, assault, arson, and even murder occurred. Property damage topped fifty billion dollars, and dozens of people lost their lives. Later, at a federal trial, two of the officers were found guilty and sent to prison. But the damage had already been done. The state's decision had triggered racial unrest within the Los Angeles community, and it quickly swept across the country.

King's question may have come across as rhetorical to many cynical late-night comedians, but to those who live out Jesus' command to love your neighbor as yourself, King's question, "Can't we all get along?" is one they answer every day of their lives. Reconcilers live by the uncompromising perspective that racial unity will happen only when each person takes full responsibility for improving the world. Imagine that: Rodney King — the victim — saw peacemaking and reconciliation as *his* personal responsibility. Until you take ownership of the global problem of racial justice and bridge building, you will not be motivated to leave your comfort zone.

I was able to formulate two penetrating questions about community building from reading the book *The Different Drum* by M. Scott Peck.[2] They are: "Why are we together?" and "How are we to be together?" These questions recognize that the bedrock of any just civilization is the strength of its community, which rests upon the strength of its citizens.

The question *Why are we together?* calls us to individually examine our mission as a community. It forces us to dig down to the core of our collective identity to understand that every human being searches for meaning and value in life. The common values of security, health, opportunity, shelter, and a sense of belonging must be made equally available to all, despite racial or ethnic differences. Living in community with one another ensures that these common denominators are safeguarded.

The question *How are we to be together?* addresses the ethical and moral side of our actions. We cannot experience true community with one another without creating and maintaining fair and equitable rules that guide our treatment of one another. If our treatment toward one another favors one ethnic group over another, we cannot achieve true community.

This is the very reason why many within the African-American community of Los Angeles rioted in response to the state court's ruling. The public viewed the evidence as indisputable and felt that no one should have been treated the way King was, regardless of the crime. The videotaped recording of the beating by a private citizen showed that the police officers used excessive force in arresting King, and the ruling in favor of the officers' acquittals sent the message that it was acceptable for white police officers to brutalize members of the black community. The rioters *and* the federal court overturned the state's ruling.

WHAT'S YOUR ROLE IN ALL OF THIS?

Rodney King's 1991 beating may seem far removed from your life today, but it's important to note that the riot was caused when the individual's view became the collective view of many. One person's view snowballed with another person's until their individual views became the singular view of the community.

Riots and injustices begin with individuals, not communities. Similarly, living in community with others begins with individuals and not communities. Your cultural comfort zone can become a dangerous place for you and anyone who is different from you, as it isolates you from them. Our comfort zones can prompt us to change if we recognize their limitations and do something about them.

A world without reconcilers who value people living in community means a world without fully practicing disciples of Jesus Christ. Our individual values form the foundation of how we portray the Christian faith. Racial reconciliation is everyone's responsibility. It starts with you and me! Your view can help shape our collective view. Breaking through your comfort zone will cause others to do the same.

This is exactly what Roger Bannister's triumph did for

other runners. In 1954, Bannister broke the world record by running the mile in less than four minutes. No one had ever done that before. This was a feat that most people had considered impossible, although some runners came fairly close. Surprisingly, within six weeks of Bannister's breaking this psychological and physical barrier, the four-minute mile was broken again by another runner: John Landy of Australia. And within a couple of years, it was broken hundreds of times.

This story affirms my point: When we break through barriers, whether cultural or racial, it will help others do the same. This will ultimately lead to global change. I am convinced that if every Christian took personal ownership of the call to become a reconciler, we could change the world. Global reconciliation starts with individuals who assume personal responsibility for change.

CHAPTER 2

WHERE DO YOU STAND?

've taught on the Bible passage that captures Jesus' rebuke "You cannot serve both God and money" in many parts of the world, from Australia to Africa to South America and even in the USA. But I've never met a self-proclaimed money worshipper. No one ever announces, "I worship money. Money is my god."

Yet in every setting where I've taught that passage, several people present fit the profile. They worshipped money. If I surveyed the wives in the room, some would surely say, "Yep, my husband is a worshipper of money. I've often seen him pay tribute to it." If I asked the husbands whether their wives worshipped money, many would certainly respond, "Yes! All this woman speaks about is money. Money is her god."

But people labeled worshippers of money usually can't see it. They'd likely want to come to blows at the insult of being called a money lover. Similarly, people who hold racial prejudices don't often realize it. Someone else must "out" them. That means that you might not be the best person to judge your own cross-cultural appeal. Ask yourself, *Do I have any friends outside of my race?* If not, why not? And take it a step further by examining the kinds of people you allow to become emotionally close to you.

Perhaps others are put off by the overarching role your ethnicity plays in your life. Don't get me wrong; I'm not saying that your heritage shouldn't be celebrated. You have every right to be proud of your Mexican roots or your Italian ancestry. If you can trace your family tree back to the *Mayflower*, that's great. What I am saying is that when you build your life around your ethnicity, it goes beyond celebration to becoming the focal point of your worship. Remember, God is a jealous God. He wants to be the sole object of everyone's worship.

Let's get back to my question about whether you have cross-race friends. If not, it may be due to prejudice or, at best, an imbalance in the role your ethnicity plays in your life. The sociologist C. H. Dodd said that ethnicity is a "group classification often based on one's physical, linguistic, or national heritage."[1] Ethnicity includes features like skin color, hereditary marks such as hair color and texture, and a shared common ancestry.

If someone from another race or culture walked into your house, would they feel welcome? Perhaps your home is adorned with art and wall hangings that showcase your ethnicity. You may think that's pretty harmless, but it doesn't stop there. What about your collection of books? Do the majority of the topics on your shelves reflect your ethnic background? Would your guest find few authors of different races represented there? Check out your Facebook and other social network pages. Are your friends all of the same race or ethnicity? What if someone from a different race sat down alongside you and listened to the music in your iPod? Would they feel included or excluded by your choices? Are

your favorite TV shows representative of a single culture
—yours?

You get the picture. When our private world centers on
our ethnicity and plays a leading role in our lives, sociologists
characterize our behavior as ethnocentric. I call it an open
door to prejudice. While I'm in no way condemning the value
of knowing and loving your heritage, there is a difference
between taking pride in your race and being consumed by it.

Where do you stand? Are you ethnocentric or
ethno-conscious?

ETHNOCENTRIC OR ETHNO-CONSCIOUS?

Ethnocentric people avoid being outside their own heritage.
People who are *ethno-conscious* appreciate their culture and
ethnicity but are not limited by it nor dominated by a need to
position it as the cornerstone in their lives. They are aware of
and at peace with their ethnicity. To be ethno-conscious is to
be comfortable with the skin you live in. Tiger Woods is a
good example of an ethno-conscious person. He jokingly calls
himself a "cablinasian" as a conscious acknowledgment of his
mixed ethnicity, which includes Caucasian, African-American,
Asian, and American Indian.

Living an ethno-conscious life is more than a phase in
your development or a back-to-your-roots season in your life.
It is an acknowledgment to yourself and to the world that you
know exactly what your ethnicity is and that you're aware of
how others have identified you. Whether you agree with their
labeling or not, you have come to terms with how you define
and identify your ethnicity.

YOU CANNOT SERVE BOTH GOD AND ETHNICITY!

No one's life can have more than one center, which is why ethnocentric individuals struggle to put Christ first in their lives. Jesus said it this way: "No one can serve two masters. Either he will hate the one and love the other, or he will be devoted to the one and despise the other. You cannot serve both God and Money" (Matthew 6:24). I would paraphrase the last sentence of this verse this way: "You cannot serve both God and ethnicity!" Jesus challenged us to choose between our devotion to Him and our devotion to money. Similarly, we must choose between our devotion to Him and our devotion to our race and culture.

Just as you can't be God-centered and money-centered, you can't be consumed with your race and remain devoid of prejudiced attitudes. Because of its inherent slant and racial bias, an ethnocentric worldview produces weaker cross-race relationships. In contrast, because of the inherent value of inclusion, the ethno-conscious perspective has the potential to form significantly stronger cross-race relationships.

The great apostle Paul acknowledged his own ethno-consciousness when he described himself as being "circumcised on the eighth day, of the people of Israel, of the tribe of Benjamin, a Hebrew of Hebrews; in regard to the law, a Pharisee" (Philippians 3:5). He makes no bones about what he looked like, his ancestral tree, his religious roots, or even his national heritage. Yet Paul did not allow his ethnic identification card to be the center of his life. Being a Jew—or, as he put it, a Hebrew of Hebrews—did not stand front and center as the primary focal point in his life.

The way we frame our concept of race relations is firmly founded upon how we identify ourselves and whether we define our ethnicity as the cornerstone of our lives. Is your ethnicity the cornerstone of your life? Or is your Creator—the One who made you—the cornerstone of your life? In Philippians 3, verses 4 and 7, Paul placed his ethnicity *beneath* his relationship with Christ: "If anyone else thinks he has reasons to put confidence in the flesh, I have more. . . . But whatever was to my profit I now consider loss for the sake of Christ." Paul had chosen to make all the ethnic identifiers he listed subservient to his role as a Christ follower. To be a Christian, Paul had to be Christ-centered in his new identity and how he viewed the world.

Paul's decision to live a Christ-centered life was a purposeful move acknowledging that his ethnic identity should not be his focus. Similarly, your ethnic identity should not be the central theme around which everything in your life orbits.

A recent speaking engagement in New Zealand exposed me to the unique ministry of one of the local professors who was of aboriginal descent. The entire world has mourned the historic treatment of the aboriginal people at the hands of Europeans who migrated to Australia and New Zealand. During the period of 1492 through the 1950s, the violence and genocide against them has resulted in physical, cultural, economic, social, and psychological trauma that still has an impact even today.

After my session that night at the conference, Professor Hume made his way toward me as I was relaxing in the greenroom. He told me that my talk on the role of God in culture was right up his alley. He mentioned that he travels within the aboriginal community and among other ethnic groups globally who have also suffered from ethnic cleansing, promoting healing and teaching reconciliation. He said that this ministry assignment was born out of God's healing him emotionally and psychologically of the self-hatred that stemmed from the brutalization of his people. He noted that most of the remaining aboriginals struggle with learned helplessness triggered by a self-hatred of their own ethnicity.

Professor Hume helps these groups avoid becoming ethnocentric by teaching them to become reconciled to God through Jesus Christ, to become reconciled to others by loving their neighbor as they love themselves, and to learn to love themselves because they have been fearfully and wonderfully made in the image of God. These unique insights on the threefold dimension of reconciliation come out of Paul's second letter to the Corinthian church (see 2 Corinthians 5:17-21). My brief interaction with Professor Hume confirmed to me once again that an ethno-conscious outlook provides grounds for healing and cross-cultural growth.

God gave us our race and ethnicity to enjoy over a lifetime. But when our ethnicity becomes our primary focus, preoccupying our thoughts and fueling our passions, like NASA scientists we must conclude, "Houston, we have a problem!" Remember, you will not have satisfying cross-cultural relationships if you are consumed with your ethnicity or choose to remain silent on interracial matters.

STATE YOUR POSITION IN FAVOR OF DIVERSITY

It's extremely important to put your beliefs on the record. Taking such a bold step removes all ambiguity about your values, beliefs, position, and expected course of action regarding race relations. This defining moment is extremely critical in the lives of true reconcilers.

On a number of occasions, I have been privately approached by individuals seeking coaching tips on how to address a touchy personal issue associated with a person of another race. Invariably, when I ask why they didn't confront the problem directly, the answer is almost always the same: "I don't want to be perceived as being prejudiced." Most often they tell me that they believed that the problem person would be quick to label anything awkward between them as a racial or ethnic bias and that they felt they lacked the insight to tackle the problem on their own, even if it had nothing to do with race. The answer in most cases was obvious to me: They had neglected to clearly state their position in favor of diversity, making them vulnerable in this area.

In such cases, my advice is always the same: Tackle the problem head-on by indicating upfront that this is not a racial issue but rather one associated with the problem person's character. In other words, let this problem be your defining moment as a cross-cultural ambassador for Christ. There is no better time to lay down your position in favor of diversity than during a conflict. If you sidestep the issue or delegate it to an associate, you will never establish your own authority regarding matters of race within the organization or work group, and you will never have the authority to address future interracial conflicts, which are sure to arise in any racially mixed setting. A person in this situation must seize the moment and put his or her position on the record.

While studying a growing congregation in California with more than sixty different nationalities, I learned that the white pastor had marched with Dr. Martin Luther King Jr. during the civil rights movement. He had also publicly addressed a sticky issue regarding an interracial romance that had formed between an African-American boy and a white girl in the congregation during the 1970s, a time when the flock was enjoying its unique racial mix. But the budding interracial romance was creating unanticipated complications. While the black families were a bit more accepting of the relationship, the girl's family and other white families in the church did not condone her choice. The pastor did not allow this sensitive matter to fester in private conversations among pockets of church members. He refused to label the interracial romance as wrong or shortsighted, and sadly, some of the whites left the church. By the time I came to interview him, this pastor was clear that his stated position in these two earlier matters — the civil rights march and his acceptance of interracial relationships — had earned him the authority to speak into racial situations within his church and local community.

People who struggle to put their position toward diversity on the line will have little authority and only marginal success in bringing about reconciliation. Reconcilers gain when they put their positions on the record. The key is to put your position on the record before a problem surfaces.

VOTE WITH YOUR FEET

With tears streaming down their faces, a middle-aged white couple approached me after my sermon to say, "We've decided to join Christ Church because our former church doesn't embrace diversity. It is 100 percent white." As Fran and John shared their hearts, I learned that in the past few years, they had felt a growing burden to adopt minority children. More specifically, this childless couple desired to adopt siblings. And they wanted their church home to reflect diversity — a place where the kids would fit in and feel a sense of belonging. So, without burning bridges, Fran and John voted with their feet by graciously transitioning their membership from their former church.

Being married for almost thirty years to Marlinda has caused me to pick up some of her habits. Like Marlinda, I now find myself asking married couples how they first met. I put the question to Phyllis and Paul, an interracial couple. She is white with blonde hair and blue eyes, and he is Korean-American with jet-black hair and a chiseled muscular frame. They met at college, where they both found the Lord through the Christian ministry on campus. Both came from Christian families, so the excitement about their respective conversions was tremendous—a clear answer to the prayers of their parents. Paul grew up in a single-parent household and had never met his father. Phyllis came from the more traditional family structure; both her mother and father lived at home and were actively involved in raising the children. Phyllis's parents strongly opposed her interracial relationship and refused to meet Paul. And Paul's mother refused to meet Phyllis, which was odd to him, as her two best friends were white and she'd raised him to not be prejudiced. She was also a member of a multiracial church.

This couple had been married some thirty-five years, but I could feel the pain of what they'd encountered at the inception of their relationship. Phyllis spoke up, saying, "After some months and much convincing by Paul, his mother, Alice, finally invited me for dinner at her home. I was very nervous and didn't know what to expect. I desperately wanted her approval, especially since my parents had decided that they would never accept Paul. During dinner, Alice began warming up to me."

Phyllis went on to say that years later, these were Alice's exact words about that night: "My preconceived ideas of you disappeared right there at the dinner table. And I had to repent to God because I immediately knew that a stand for diversity cannot be only a Sunday-morning expression of faith; it had to run throughout the course of my entire life." Phyllis continued, "We wept together. Alice became a mom to me, especially during those early years of my marriage when my own mother emotionally withdrew her affection because of my having a Korean husband. Looking back through the eyes of Scripture, I would equate my relationship with Alice to that of Ruth and Naomi — they were inseparable in love, affection toward one another, and friendship."

In order for healthy cross-race relationships to form in your life, you must take a public stance that is undeniably pro-diversity. Alice took a true stance and Phyllis's parents joined her, albeit years later when the grandchildren came along. Without credibility, becoming a reconciler would be an impossible task.

THE POWER OF CREDIBILITY

In the 2010 movie *Sins of the Mother*, Shay Hunter, a struggling graduate student played by Nicole Beharie, is forced to return home to live with her mother, from whom she has been estranged for a number of years. She has no job, no place to live, and no one else to turn to. She is so deeply troubled and emotionally damaged that she periodically pulls her hair out in response to the emotional pain she has experienced since childhood. Her mother, Nona, played by Jill Scott, was an alcoholic and had shared her bed with all kinds of men. Nona had slept in her own vomit and fallen into a myriad of painful, drunken ordeals. As a child, Shay witnessed these things and had to mother her mother rather than be mothered by her.

When she returns home, Shay is surprised to find that Nona is now a recovering alcoholic practicing the twelve-step recovery process religiously. But Shay is suspicious of Nona and finds it difficult to interact respectfully with her. In fact, she's even unwilling to call her Mom. She simply relates to Nona by her first name. To Shay, Nona has zero credibility. She believes that Nona is merely pretending to be a recovering alcoholic. She's waiting for the old Nona, the real Nona, the disappointing Nona to show up again.

The scene that establishes Nona's credibility is the Sunday morning that she invites Shay to attend church with her. Nona is scheduled to stand up in front of the congregation and tell her story—to give a testimony—of how God had brought her from the depths of her alcoholism by His grace. Nona gives a beautiful testimony of the goodness of God, but it only irritates Shay. Nona's daughter wants her mother to tell the church members how she used to be and about the pain she had brought upon herself and her daughter. Nona's testimony conveniently leaves out that part of her past and focuses only on the comeback portion of her journey. Too angry to contain her emotions, Shay makes a huge outburst in the middle of the church service, demanding honesty and credibility from Nona.

Nona tearfully walks off the platform and stands in the aisle, looking at her angry daughter. Amid sobs, Nona breaks down and says to Shay in front of the entire congregation, "I hated myself for what I did to you." Shay yells back, "This is not about you!" The heated interchange continues with Nona saying, "How many times must I say I'm sorry?" Nona breaks down even further with deeper sobs this time and tells her daughter with great humility, "I'm agreeing with you." The emotional exchange and Nona's tearful expression conveys this reality: "I'm not fighting you. I hurt you, and I hurt because I hurt you. I'm terribly sorry."

At that moment, Nona sees that she has achieved credibility in her daughter's eyes. Shay no longer needs her mother to prove herself. She sees that Nona, too, has become emotionally empty. She knows that all that is left is a broken woman who had no other recourse but to genuinely admit to her daughter, "My past struggle with alcohol has devastated you emotionally. I'm sorry."

At its lowest common denominator, credibility reflects honesty of the deepest kind, an honesty that stems from the heart. Without credibility, your relationships can't be healthy. Without credibility, you can't develop cross-cultural relationships. No matter who you are, you are not exempt from being called on the carpet when your credibility looks suspect.

We saw this during the 2008 presidential elections when the Reverend Jeremiah Wright came to the forefront as candidate Obama's pastor. When some of his inflammatory quotes were released to the news media in the midst of the election, the nation took special notice. He reportedly said, "In the twenty-first century, white America got a wake-up call after 9/11/01. White America and the western world came to realize that people of color had not gone away, faded into the woodwork, or just 'disappeared' as the Great White West kept on its merry way of ignoring black concerns."[2] The American public had every right to demand an answer from Obama. If he really was a true reconciler, why did he maintain his membership at

Trinity United Church of Christ under the controversial Wright?

Over the twenty years Barack Obama held membership in the congregation, Wright had repeatedly made biased statements. Both Republicans and nonpartisans demanded that Mr. Obama address this issue. Most Americans felt that Obama's membership at Trinity United meant that he condoned the flagrant hate-laced speeches of his minister. Because he held membership in a church adhering to such a racially divisive theology and worldview, many questioned his role as an authentic reconciler.

In order to be credible as a reconciler, Senator Obama had to vote with his feet. He resigned his membership and publicly distanced himself from Wright. This action alone wasn't enough to secure the senator's position as a reconciler though. Mr. Obama had to publicly state *his* position on the matter of race. This requirement was met on March 18, 2008, when he delivered his famous "A More Perfect Union" speech from the Constitution Center in Philadelphia. The speech expressed his heart on the matter of race in America. No longer was his position in favor of diversity going to be called into question. With this speech, Obama effectively prevented Wright's racially divisive sermons from darkening his image.

Credibility conveys the idea that a person is honest, upright, and ethical. When the American Management Association asked 1,500 managers nationwide, "What values (personal traits or characteristics) do you look for in your superiors?" the number one answer was *honesty*. Honesty was then best described as credibility.[3] People are looking for credibility in those they choose to follow. This is especially important in multiracial settings.

Credibility has to do with letting others know where they stand with you. It also means carrying yourself above reproach by being aboveboard in your word and conduct. State your position regarding your appreciation and value of diversity. Be sure that others know where they stand because you've told them yourself.

TAKE COURAGE

Living as a reconciler requires taking a firm stance, privately and publicly. This is exactly what Billy Graham had to do during his 1997 crusade when his private value that all people are important to God and, accordingly, must be important to me was challenged.[4] Cognizant of the large Hispanic and Catholic population living in and around the San Antonio region, Graham intentionally held a huge outreach targeting their community. He formed a strategic alliance with Archbishop Patrick Flores, a Mexican-American priest who served as the highest-ranking Catholic clergyman in Texas. Together, they taped radio spots in English and Spanish, encouraging people to attend the crusade to develop a closer relationship with Jesus Christ.

But Billy Graham's commitment to evangelize across cultural lines unnerved some people who did not share that same passion. Some fundamentalists even criticized his cross-cultural approach by posting fliers in downtown San Antonio featuring Graham in a clerical collar with the caption "Reject Billy Graham—He's Too Catholic." Despite the opposition's efforts, the four-day crusade drew a crowd of some 247,500 people. For the first time in its then three-year history, the Alamodome was filled nightly.

Dr. Graham shared his position on the need to be intentionally cross-cultural when he said in his opening sermon, "The Devil has separated us, and a crusade like this is used of God to bring people of all denominations together. . . . We need one another."[5] Thousands of Latinos made decisions for Christ. The crusade's success in penetrating the Latino community can be attributed to one man's unwavering commitment to living cross-culturally, even in the face of naysayers.

It takes courage to publically voice your agreement in favor of diversity. If you hope to have any influence in today's racially diverse society, you have to wear your courage like a well-tailored suit: with confidence and pride.

Self-confidence stems from knowing you've adopted the right position. How can loving and embracing other races be wrong? How can wanting the best for every race be considered an incorrect perspective? It would be silly for anyone to consider your positive opinion detrimental to the betterment of society. You have every reason in the world to square your shoulders with self-confidence and pride.

Like a five-year-old ring bearer dressed fashionably in a black-and-white tuxedo, square your shoulders and walk proudly down the center aisle to the altar — the place where vows and commitments are made for life. Your new life is about to begin — a life committed to building relationships across cultural lines. Take pride in obeying Jesus' command to love your neighbor as yourself. It's the right thing to do! You will not be disappointed.

CHAPTER 3

WHAT BRINGS PEOPLE TOGETHER?

I am not a basketball player, the son of a basketball player, or even a basketball fan, so I was surprised when the Lord opened the door for me to help international players get connected with their American teammates within the NBA and American culture. A week before my talk with these rookies, I was racking my brain about what to say, how to reach them, how to empower them with information that would help them connect with each other. *There must be a common denominator that will bring these guys together*, I thought.

The words of sports commentator Henry Abbott echoed in my head: "There's no room for prejudice on winning teams. And if some other guy from some other country with some other skin color is doing it better? Well, then it's that guy's time to shine, even if he doesn't look like you."[1] His words gave me an idea. I decided to create a game. Because athletes love winning and basketball players are no different, I wanted to create a game-like situation that would bring people together and build a supportive community. I created two teams, one called the "Red Team" and the other the "Blue Team."

We were not on a basketball court. This game was going to be played in a meeting room without a basketball. I assigned two points and three points, the same scoring system as for a basketball game, to the questions I was going to ask each team. The questions centered on the flight time of the international players' arrival into New York City from their respective parts of the world. It made sense. The dozen or so international players took turns sharing the names of their countries while others assigned to their team guessed the flying time to the Big Apple. The room was charged with testosterone. The guys were engaged. Laughter, fun, high fives, and even some frustration brought the teammates together. And the harmless but spirited competition even brought the respective teams together.

What I took away from this modest exercise was this: People get together across cultural, racial, and even national lines when they share the same need, goal, prize, or struggle.

WHAT'S IN IT FOR ME?

The short answer to the question *What brings people together?* is economics. When I use the word *economics*, I don't necessarily mean money; I mean value or benefit. In essence, people from diverse backgrounds come together in a set place at a set time because they benefit from something personally valuable. Sociologists call this dynamic the social exchange theory. People from every racial background will go wherever they have to in order to reap the benefits they seek.

Think about it. Why do shopping centers, food stores, department of motor vehicle (DMV) offices, voting halls, and other places such as schools and large corporate offices attract a racially diverse group? People gather in those places because their needs can be met at only these places. The malls meet our need for new clothing and other essentials, and the supermarket meets our need to buy food. Whatever our race or ethnicity, we all need to go to the DMV if we want the appropriate documents authorizing us to drive. If we want an education, especially an official degree accompanied by an official transcript, we have to go to college. Economics is king!

You must focus on this principle if you want to understand how cross-racial relationships are formed and maintained, especially if you desire to lead a diverse team in the workplace or community. You must offer some recognizable social benefit that reaches across racial lines. People connect with others when the personal benefits to be gained are greater than the discomfort that might result from establishing a cross-race relationship. Economically speaking, the assets must outweigh the liabilities.

This principle was at the heart of why Jessica, a white, and Louise, an African-American, became fast friends. Jessica grew up in an all-white community in the hills of West Virginia. She told me, "Not only were there no other races around us, my father was the consummate bigot, like the old sitcom character Archie Bunker of *All in the Family*. My dad would warn me whenever he saw people of different races during our monthly trips to the big city, 'Stay away from them. They are no good. All they do is complain about whites hurting them or not giving them a fair shake,'" she said.

The first time she had to be around an African-American was when she began working. Louise, her coworker, was friendly, but Jessica still remained guarded and suspicious.

Even though she was a Christian at that point, her father's poison was still in her system. She went on to say, "As I settled into the job, I knew I had to tell at least one person that I was battling a disease that caused me to pass out anywhere at anytime for no apparent reason. I later learned that I had the rare disease called neurocardiogenic syncope, which, due to periodic low blood circulation to the brain, would result in seizure-like symptoms and fainting spells. This would happen sometimes when I was driving or just sitting down somewhere. It was quite dangerous. Without anyone else to confide in, I turned to Louise out of desperation and told her about my illness and what to do if that ever happened at work. She sympathetically listened and smiled, saying, 'God and I will help you, sweetheart.'"

About three weeks later, Jessica was sitting in the conference room next to Louise when she passed out and slumped over the chair, immobile. When she came to, she was sitting in the emergency room with Louise and the doctors looking down on her. Louise had quickly sprung into action and called 911. An ambulance rushed to the job site and whisked Jessica off to the hospital. With tears welling up in her eyes, Jessica said, "Louise, my first African-American friend, saved my life." Their friendship continued to blossom from there. They went shopping together and ate dinner at each other's homes with their families.

People connect with others because of a perceived benefit. Jessica's medical needs required that she reach out to a caring coworker, but the benefit can be expressed as simply as, "Being around you makes me feel more confident about myself."

This principle of "What's in it for me?" may appear to be a bit self-serving, but there is a mutual benefit because both parties profit from the relationship. When you go to the super-market, the grocer gets your money and you get food, right? You both benefit from the exchange. Neither action is viewed as being selfish.

If you want to thrive in building cross-race friendships, you must embrace this perspective. Don't ignore the reality that people connect with those who benefit them in some way.

THE GRACE OF GOD

Because cross-race relationships are extremely important to God, we must consider the role He plays in bringing them about. A little phrase in Acts 11:23 provides the answer: "When [Barnabas] arrived and saw evidence of *the grace of God*, he was glad and encouraged them all to remain true to the Lord with all their hearts" (emphasis added). This passage captures the historical account following the stoning of the first Christian martyr, Stephen, as he spoke openly against the Jewish leaders who stood in strong opposition to the message of Jesus being the messiah. After Stephen's brutal murder, many Christians abandoned Jerusalem — the place of the crime — in fear of their lives. Some came to Antioch, where they apprehensively continued to share their faith. The displaced disciples, some hailing from cross-cultural cities such as Cyprus and Cyrene, openly evangelized among the Jews and Greeks (see Acts 11:19-26).

To everyone's surprise, both Greeks and Jews came to Christ. For the first time in the history of the New Testament era, a cross-cultural church was birthed. Jews and Greeks freely participated in the worship community. When this news reached the apostles in Jerusalem, they sent Barnabas — a

cross-cultural leader—to this accidentally planted multicultural church. Barnabas entered the room where a diverse crowd
of people were connecting with one another around the person
of Jesus Christ and said that it was the grace of God that
accomplished this.

Bible teacher James Ryle explains that "grace is the empowering presence of God enabling you to be who God created
you to be, and to do what God has called you to do."[2] In other
words, the things that seem too hard to do and too difficult to
become can be achieved only with the help of God's grace.
The diversity experienced at Antioch was made possible
through the grace of God. The cross-race relationships that
were formed despite the historic tension between Jews and
Greeks were made possible, not through political correctness
or some slick cross-cultural technique for making friends but
by the grace of God. God had supernaturally empowered His
people to act like His people and do the things His people
were called to do. This is what we need today! We need the
grace of God to help us live, act, think, and do the things Jesus
called us to do.

The peculiar thing about God's grace is that the only way
to activate it is to rest in His ability. The believers in the early
church were running for their lives, and they arrived at
Antioch looking for a safe haven. God's grace was triggered as
they shared their faith. Despite fears, basic life, and needs,
evangelism is always the right thing to do. It is the highest
form of demonstrating love to those bound for a Christ-less
eternity. And as these early believers did the right thing,
people responded.

Victoria Ruvolo also experienced God's grace as she did
the right thing when everything else would have been easily

justifiable. Ryan Cushing, a teenager, had thrown a twenty-pound frozen turkey onto Victoria's car's windshield. The turkey bent her car's steering wheel inward, smashed her face, and broke every bone it touched. In his book *Captured by Grace*, David Jeremiah completes the story.

On Monday August 15, 2005, Ryan Cushing met his victim Victoria Ruvolo, the forty-four-year-old Long Island woman whom he had damaged from a teenage prank. He was no longer tough but broken and emptied of the teenage tough-guy image.

He pled guilty of the crime. However, he received "a trifling six months behind bars, five years probation, a bit of counseling, a dash of public service." The angry public decried the lenient punishment. The victim had to endure her eye being affixed by a synthetic film, her face stapled together by titanium plates, a wired jaw, and a tracheotomy.

The reason for the light sentence? Victoria had asked for it. When Ryan heard the judge's response to the victim's cry, he wept with abandon as his attorney led him over to Victoria. She "holds him tight, comforts him, strokes his hair, and offers reassuring words. 'I forgive you,' she whispers. 'I want your life to be the best it can be.'"

The New York Times dubbed it "a moment of grace."[3]

How was Victoria able to freely forgive Ryan for such a vicious act that permanently disabled her? How were Greeks and Jews able to worship Jesus together in Antioch? How will you learn to build healthy cross-racial relationships when it seems so hard? Only by the grace of God! Grace happens when you move toward the action requested by God. He requested that the early church walk and live in love, even in the face of martyrdom; He requested that Victoria forgive

Ryan; and He requests that you love your neighbor as yourself (see Luke 10:27).

While economics and the grace of God are part of the reason people get together, they are not the only factors. There are things we can do to increase the likelihood of establishing interracial friendships. Let's explore what those practices are.

BRINGING PEOPLE TOGETHER ACROSS RACIAL LINES

Patty, an African-American woman, shared an interesting cross-cultural experience with me. She had recently returned from a business trip to China. The Chinese girls she encountered were mesmerized with her skin color and hair texture. They had never seen an African-American person before. In their broken English, they asked permission to touch Patty's skin and her hair, and, being a teacher, Patty obliged. The girls giggled as they learned what a black person's hair feels like. Patty returned the friendly gesture by stroking their hair and touching their skin. They laughed even louder because they didn't see anything unusual about their skin or hair texture. But they thanked Patty for allowing them to touch her.

Patty and the children were onto something. They all instinctively modeled the five practices that bring people together across cultural and racial lines. These practices are:

1. Act neighborly.
2. Share common interests.
3. Be warm and inviting.
4. Offer mutual respect.
5. Respond with kindness.

1. Act neighborly.

Neighbors are people who are geographically close to us, which was the case with Patty and the Chinese girls. She was in their nation, in their backyard, so to speak. Interracial relationships occur when people of different races have a chance to interact with one another up close. When you spend time in places where there are people of other races — whether at work, school, or the gym — your daily routine increases the likelihood that you will connect with them in a social way.

If people outside your race are not part of your routine comings and goings, you need to tweak your lifestyle to widen your social base. Perhaps you can volunteer at a community hospital, local fire department, civic organization, or even your neighborhood watch committee. Maybe you can establish your gym membership in a more racially diverse part of town. You will be surprised by the number of people you can meet when you choose to broaden your social circle.

2. Share common interests.

Girls all over the world take a personal interest in their hair; they want it to look attractive and well groomed. The Chinese girls were fascinated by the different texture of the black woman's hair and asked, "Can we touch your hair?" Patty recognized how universal hair is to women, and she wanted the girls to feel equally important in this cross-cultural exercise, so she asked to feel their hair too. They were sharing a common interest.

Similarity plays a pivotal role in friendship formation. It is the basis of interpersonal attraction, as is evidenced when you hear such things as "You remind me of my favorite teacher" or "You remind me of my kid brother." We form friendships with people from other cultures when we look beyond race for commonalities. Relationships are formed on shared values and interests.

3. Be warm and inviting.

Instead of responding negatively to the Chinese girls' request to touch her hair, Patty was warm and inviting. She knew that they were simply curious. And, as kids, they didn't see any harm in speaking their minds to a total stranger.

If you want to have friends who are culturally different from you, you must be warm and inviting in every area of your life that gives other cultures access to you. It's true on an individual level, and it's also true on an organizational level. This includes the organizations where you hold memberships and affiliations, even your church and job.

Rebecca, a Latina of Dominican descent, worked in the community development division for a national organization for girls and traveled throughout the United States. On a trip to Montana, she found herself in a town where the people were cold toward outsiders, particularly nonwhites. She was there over the weekend and while watching television saw a church with a spiritually uplifting program. When the pastor invited all viewers to attend one of their weekend services, she decided to go there on Sunday for worship.

Because the church was in a small Montana community, she did not expect a lot of diversity, but Rebecca's commitment to modeling authentic Christianity gave her the courage to be the only nonwhite worshipper that day. She arrived at the service a little late and sat toward the rear of the auditorium. The congregation worshipped with excitement and energy. During worship, the pastor walked by her as he headed down the aisle toward the platform. When he saw her out of the corner of his eye, he suddenly stopped and gruffly asked her, "Why are you here?" Shocked, Rebecca responded, "I saw you on television this morning and I wanted to worship with your church." Without saying another word, the minister continued walking toward the altar.

When it came time to acknowledge first-time visitors, the host said, "All first-time visitors please stand so that we can greet you and present you with one of our visitor packets." Rebecca and a number of other visitors — all white — rose to their feet. Everyone was warmly handed a visitor packet — everyone but Rebecca.

With a sad smile on her face, Rebecca told me what happened when she walked to the information desk to retrieve her visitor packet at the end of the service. "The young lady turned her head away from me, stepped back a couple of feet, and with a visitor packet in hand stretched as far as she could to hand it to me without touching any part of my person. I was shocked. I was not welcomed there by anyone."

Sadly, this church had no desire to foster diversity. If you are going to develop friends across racial lines, you have to be warm and inviting to everybody.

4. Offer mutual respect.

When the Chinese girls asked Patty's permission to touch her hair, they were also offering her the mutual respect everyone deserves. They did not put her on a lower social level. She was their equal, and they recognized that offering her mutual respect was *their* responsibility. Offering respect to others, especially those who are different from us, demonstrates that we see ourselves as their social equal. This practice is inescapable if you want to establish cross-cultural relationships.

Adults sometimes struggle with this behavior. Although we live in a nation where racially biased hiring practices and discriminatory employee treatment is illegal, our culture often stifles an appreciation for diversity. We see this in the perceived status of minorities. Status is a personal issue, but it becomes a societal concern when it comes to placing someone in a position of influence over others. The subtle assumptions you make when you meet a person for the first time tells a lot about how you perceive their status in relation to yours.

Whites in America have enjoyed some historical benefits tied to being in the majority, and they may have to work harder at identifying how well they implement this practice. Most whites are unconsciously blind to their bias. For example, a three-year undercover investigation by the National Fair Housing Alliance found that real estate agents steered whites away from integrated neighborhoods and steered African-Americans toward predominantly black neighborhoods.[4]

Dr. Jack Dovidio, a professor at the University of Connecticut, has researched racism for more than thirty years. He estimates that up to 80 percent of white Americans have racist feelings they may not even recognize. Dovidio shared, "We've reached a point that racism is like a virus that has mutated into a new form that we don't recognize." He added that twenty-first-century racism is different from that of the past. "Contemporary racism is not conscious, and it is not accompanied by dislike, so it gets expressed in indirect, subtle ways," he said.[5]

Discriminatory behavior shows a blatant disrespect for individuals and families who should be given equal opportunity to live in the neighborhoods of their choice.

Here are two questions to determine whether you offer mutual respect to others.

- Do you automatically assume that someone of a different race is lower on the status totem pole than you are?
- Do you take on a teacher-like tone when speaking to someone of a different race because you assume you know more than the other person?

Please don't breeze through these questions. Your answers can lead to an experience with the Holy Spirit that results in your dropping to your knees in repentance. Don't miss this opportunity to use this time of reflection and introspection.

How do you see yourself when you look through the lens of social status? How do you see people who are racially different from you? If you really want to know the answer, ask someone of another race with whom you've formed a friendship and ask a peer. Don't ask someone who is significantly older or younger than you or who is your superior or subordinate at work. An older person often comes across as a parental figure when interacting with someone younger. Likewise, a supervisor-subordinate-type relationship can easily be misconstrued as a status issue when it isn't.

So ask one or two people with whom you have a safe cross-race relationship how they perceive your interactions concerning status and mutual respect. Do they feel that you treat them as social peers, or do they feel that you automatically take the higher social position? You may want to preface this sensitive question by saying, "I have been reading a book on how to build healthy cross-cultural relationships. The author has challenged me to investigate if I offer people from other cultures mutual respect, so I'm nervously seeking your honest opinion."

If you want to build cross-cultural friendships, you must see the inherent value in everyone *before* you get to know them. You must place everyone at the same starting point when you first meet them. This action is quite validating because people of equal status respect one another's time, pay attention to each other, and ultimately benefit from one another's friendship. The highest level of validation is when you recognize the other person as someone you can learn from, despite the difference in your skin color, language, hair texture, or ethnic heritage. More important, the level of status you ascribe to others will position you as someone who can benefit from a social relationship with them; in other words, you see him or her as a potential friend.

5. Respond with kindness.

The Chinese girls thanked Patty after she allowed them to stroke her hair and feel her skin. She thanked them for allowing her to have the same reciprocal experience. Responding to someone's kindness or gesture of friendship helps stimulate an ongoing positive relationship.

People tend to be friends with those who see them as friends. If your friendly overtures toward someone are thwarted, you likely won't go out of your way to interact with that person, especially if he or she is of another race. Generally, when you greet people regularly or make other friendship gestures, you begin to engage them and get to know more about them. If there is a good exchange of questions and answers so that both people get an opportunity to share about themselves, it heightens the possibility of forming a relationship.

One Wednesday night at my Bible study group, the teaching topic was "Breaking Barriers and Building Bridges Across Racial Lines." I asked the group this question: "How many of you have not had the awesome opportunity of having someone from another race eat at your home?" Some people reluctantly raised their hands. As I trained the group over the course of the next few weeks, I gave those who had raised their hand a homework assignment. I asked them to set up a small, inexpensive dinner at their home or at a local restaurant and invite a few people from another race to join them for a meal. To help strengthen their comfort level, I allowed them to invite one other friend from our church. They had three weeks to complete the simple project.

The results were amazing. All those who participated in this cross-cultural exercise said that the awkwardness lifted and the evening flowed smoothly after a few icebreakers. And guess what? Their guests responded to their kindness and invited them to their homes for dinner. It was a win-win situation.

You can come up with a few exercises of your own to bridge the gap between you and people of other races. Granted, it will take some effort on your part, but you must break out of your routine to take advantage of the opportunity to build bridges and break down cross-cultural barriers.

LOOK AROUND YOU

Have you ever seen the 1983 movie *Trading Places*? Well, in the movie, an African-American street hustler, Billy Ray Valentine (Eddie Murphy), is unwittingly enlisted in a social experiment concocted by the Dukes, two white commodities tycoons who pluck him from the streets and put him in an executive-level job and lifestyle. The tycoons do the opposite for their soon-to-be nephew-in-law, Louis Winthorpe III (Dan Aykroyd), a white, Harvard-educated, well-heeled manager of the Dukes' firm. After a series of comical twists and turns that throw Winthorpe headfirst into the bowels of social and financial ruin while lifting Valentine to unimagined heights, the two unsuspecting "guinea pigs" learn that the Dukes had destroyed Winthorpe's status and were planning to throw Valentine back into the streets all for a one-dollar bet between them. Valentine and Winthorpe immediately put an end to the acrimony the Dukes created between them and come up with an ingenious plan to turn the tables on the tycoons. The movie ends with the Dukes penniless and on the street panhandling for their next meal while Valentine and Winthorpe sail away together as best friends on a yacht.

While this story is fictional, written and scripted by skilled Hollywood professionals, it points to the idea that forming interracial relationships is, in fact, doable, even when the parties involved are polar opposites. You may say, *That's fine for a movie, but in real life, forming these relationships—ones that provide value to both sides—takes a lot longer than two hours.* And you'd be correct. The good news is that the skills required for building cross-race relationships can be learned. And once you master them, you'll never forget them.

But you'll never build cross-race friendships if you don't make it a priority to begin looking for opportunities to connect across cultures.

Recently while driving through Jersey City—a very multiethnic community—en route to a speaking engagement, I noticed a lot of East Indians in the commercial section.

Because my eyes have been trained to see people—all kinds of people—I excitedly asked the pastor I was visiting what he and his congregation were doing to reach the sizable East Indian population within their community. His answer shocked me: "What East Indian population?" To my surprise, he had never taken notice of the thousands of Indian and Pakistani people living and working in his city because they were not *his* people. They were near, but because his heart was closed to valuing diversity, his eyes could not see them.

People of different races are walking, talking, and functioning in your world right now. They are within your sphere of influence. If you commit to asking God to help you identify potential relationships, you'll begin to see all kinds of possibilities for making friends across racial lines.

CHAPTER 4

ARE YOU RACIALLY ATTRACTIVE?

One of my favorite TV shows is *Law & Order: Special Victims Unit*. Each week, gripping real-life dramas unfold and I play armchair detective for an hour or so, riding shotgun alongside the TV cops as they unravel the whodunit details of the latest crime. As I parse through all the clues, studying the body language of potential suspects and linking the trail of evidence, I can't help but feel a bit ill at ease about one of the central characters on the show: Detective Odafin "Fin" Tutuola, played by former rapper Ice-T. Scripted as the quintessential angry black man, he has an ax to grind when it comes to race relations. His actions on the show are never prejudiced or objectionable toward whites, and it's not as though he roughs up the white suspects or mistreats his colleagues, but the bitter, sharp-edged tone in his voice leaves me feeling as if he is saying, "I'm watching you, and you better not even think about showing any racial bias toward me."

Would you be attracted to someone like that? Most likely you wouldn't. His harsh, "I'm-gonna-get-you-sucka" disposition almost invites racial conflict. People like this see a racial fire whether there is smoke or not. They can incite racial conflict from the most benign and nonracial issues. And of course it's not just blacks who harbor conspiratorial thoughts; people in every racial group have that perspective of life.

So if people like Detective Tutuola invite racial conflict, what kind of people invite racial harmony? What makes someone attractive cross-racially?

FOLLOWING JESUS' MODEL

We can learn about attracting cross-race friends by observing how Jesus behaved when interacting with non-Jews, in particular His conversation with a Samaritan woman at the well. Jesus didn't make an issue of the difference in their ethnicities, but she did. She said, "You are a Jew and I am a Samaritan woman. How can you ask me for a drink?" (John 4:9). Nor did Jesus let the social rules established by society shape His behavior. The unspoken rule of that day was that Jews do not associate with Samaritans, and vice versa. But Jesus broke the rule and freely held a conversation with the woman. His discussion about her eternal destiny demonstrated how much He valued her, despite their cultural differences.

His disciples, however, behaved like the rest of their cultural in-group. They had been on an excursion during most of His conversation with the Samaritan woman. Upon their return, they saw the two engaged in dialogue and "were surprised to find him talking with a woman. But no one asked, 'What do you want?' or 'Why are you talking with her?'" (verse 27). The disciples noted their Master's cross-cultural interchange, although they did not dare verbalize their surprise. Imagine that: You can walk with Jesus but still be uncomfortable in cross-cultural settings.

If I were a first-century reporter for the *Jerusalem Gazette*, I would have muscled my way through the crowd to interview Jesus about His behavioral traits that made Him culturally and racially attractive. But because I wasn't there and that opportunity is impossible, the next best thing was to glean answers from His twenty-first-century followers who demonstrated the same cross-cultural success. I turned again to the insights I unearthed from studying multiracial churches. These churches could not have developed diverse congregations unless a good percentage of their members connected on a personal level with someone from another race. I wanted to learn from them, so I conducted focus groups in each of the study churches around this question: "Why are people of other races attracted to you?" Their answers produced eight ways to be racially attractive:

1. Offer hospitality.
2. Be free to laugh and joke.
3. Go on social outings.
4. Engage in vulnerable conversations.
5. Have cross-race friends.
6. Seek mutually rewarding outcomes.
7. Demonstrate comfort in the friendship.
8. Practice honesty in the relationship.

Before we look carefully at each of these, I want to point out that we can see a number of these traits at work in Jesus' interaction with the Samaritan woman. His asking her for a drink of water was a surefire way to evoke *hospitality* from her. In turn, Jesus offered her Living Water. She became *vulnerable in the conversation* when He said, "Go, call your husband and come back" (John 4:16). It forced her to open up and admit, "I have no husband." With the goal of arriving at a *mutually rewarding outcome*—the salvation of her soul—Jesus addressed her moral choices without being condemning. He lovingly demonstrated *comfort in their newfound friendship* when He uncovered the fact that she'd had five husbands and the man whom she was now with was not her husband. The Samaritan woman, equally desirous for the reward of the friendship *practiced honesty in the relationship* by answering, "What you have just said is quite true" (verse 18).

Jesus modeled the very cross-cultural behavior that modern-day reconcilers have consciously or unconsciously learned to embrace as a lifestyle practice. We would do well to follow His example.

WHAT MAKES A PERSON RACIALLY ATTRACTIVE?

A truly beautiful woman does not need to draw attention to herself. She doesn't need to wear skimpy clothes or apply heavy makeup. Her striking good looks are visible to everyone she meets. Her natural beauty emanates from her person. Racial attractiveness is similar. It is natural and free-flowing. The good news is that even if it's not present in your life right now, you can learn how to have it.

As you read about these ways to become racially attractive, you may think, *I can't do that!* or *That's not who I am!* Let me assure you that all of these traits do not need to operate in your life in order for you to have cross-cultural appeal. But the more these behaviors characterize you, the stronger your cross-racial appeal will be.

You will naturally gravitate to one behavior suggestion more than another because that particular action is likely already at work in your life in some capacity; it's a natural fit with your personality and style of interaction with your same-race friends. The more you operate in a natural, free-flowing manner cross-racially, the more you are believable and can appeal to others across the human color spectrum. Let's see how you can incorporate these ideas into your life to boost your cross-cultural appeal.

1. Offer hospitality.

People who are cross-racially attractive are comfortable offering hospitality to someone of another race. Inviting someone to your home is one of the warmest gestures you can offer. It shows genuine comfort with people of other cultures, and it increases the possibility of friendship. The trait of hospitality is quite irresistible because you've made the invited guest feel welcomed, special, and wanted.

Hospitality leaves no room for guesswork. It is an inherent value to everyone, the way water is an international drink. Hospitality disarms because when it is genuine, the person offering it has no vested interest other than making you feel at ease.

Smiles, inviting body language, and words that convey warmth and acceptance are all associated with hospitality. You can easily incorporate them in order to awaken appeal across the cultural divide.

2. Be free to laugh and joke.

People who are comfortable in a cross-race relationship regularly laugh and joke in the other person's company. The humor, which sometimes is self-deprecating, creates a relaxed social atmosphere.

Humor is a universal gesture of friendship; that's why laughter cuts across racial lines so easily. I'm not referring to lewd, dirty, or racial jokes that have insult and harm at their core, nor am I talking about someone being a clown or acting as if he or she is the star at a local comedy club. I am referring to clean humor that occurs with people who know how to capture the funny things associated with everyday living. This trait provides a real benefit, especially when someone's life is filled with pain, confusion, or boredom.

I have learned over the years that some people are naturally funny while others cannot tell a joke even if they've heard it a dozen times. Humor works best when it flows naturally from your personality and everyday style. My friend Ylonda knows someone whose dad is Jewish and mother is East Indian. When Ylonda's friend meets people at parties, he often says, "People always want to know how I got a name like Emil Rosenberg—simple, I'm a HinJew." Emil's sharp wit always gets a laugh, which warms people up to him.

People with a good sense of humor, like Emil, don't lose their wit around people of other races. In the same way, a smart person cannot stop being smart, a musical person cannot stop being musical, and a scientist cannot stop thinking scientifically just because they are in the presence of someone from another race. You are what you are where you are.

3. Go on social outings.
A social setting is the litmus test for cross-cultural comfort. Most people can peacefully talk to someone of another race

in a professional setting; it is viewed as a normal part of doing business. But attending social gatherings is a choice. You let down your guard at social gatherings. You display emotions. You freely discuss likes, dislikes, and personal preferences.

So the moment you take a cross-race relationship into the public square, it moves into a whole new dimension. If you are comfortable being seen with this person in a social setting — be it at the gym, a restaurant, or a mall — your relationship has passed the invaluable comfort test. The two of you are comfortable with one another should members of your own race stare or send emotionally charged signals that ask, "Why are you hanging out with *that* person?"

When you spend time socially with someone of another race, it demonstrates that you *want* to spend time with this person. Unlike when you are at a business meeting or a staff party, a social outing is a nonbusiness, voluntary opportunity to get together.

While lounging around our living room after a Thanksgiving dinner, my youngest daughter, Jessica, shared that when she goes out with her friends, they teach her how to say her name in their mother tongue. She continued, "I know how to say, 'My name is Jessica,' in six different languages." Immediately she rattled off the phrase in Italian, Korean, German, Spanish, and Chinese. I then asked her, "Which Chinese language was that?" She said, "Mandarin." Her aunt Paula then asked, "Can you say it in Cantonese?" Jessica replied, "My Chinese friends only speak Mandarin." I vividly remembered this brief family moment because it pointed to the fact that my daughter enjoys regular social outings with her cross-race friends.

4. Engage in vulnerable conversations.

If someone answers a gnawing question that you've had for years surrounding the subject of race, an automatic heart connection can occur between you and that person. When I was a graduate student studying environmental engineering, a Korean student lived in my dormitory. We kept running into one another because of our similar schedules. He would always greet me in his broken English, and I would reciprocate. One afternoon I invited him to my room in an attempt to get to know him. I learned that he was also a Christian and was studying here in the States with the intention to go back home immediately upon graduation. We hit it off and our friendship blossomed.

I wanted to learn as much as I could about his culture and world, and he saw me as his coach regarding American culture and customs. I remember one of our meaningful discussions, in which I asked him about something that had always troubled me: "How do you tell the difference between someone who is Chinese, Japanese, or Korean?" I felt confident that he would not judge me or chastise me for my ignorance. He looked at me quizzically, as if to say, *I never thought of that before!* and responded, "I tell by the shape of their eyes. But sometimes I get it wrong." This brought me some relief.

Keep in mind that a vulnerable conversation is not an intrusive conversation in which you are prying into the life of someone you hardly know; it's a conversation similar to one you might have with an inquisitive child who innocently asks a question out of pure eagerness to learn. The motive is merely to have the knowledge to do the right thing.

If you are candid by nature, this particular trait will work well with your natural style. The next time you find yourself in a cross-race conversation, inch closer to the parameters of vulnerability and see where this leads you. You may learn that vulnerability is reciprocal. When you sow it, you will reap it. The outcome may be that you form meaningful cross-race relationships.

5. Have cross-race friends.

When you have people of other races as your friends, it is easy to form and maintain other cross-race relationships. Whenever you invite a mix of ethnicities to a social function, it sends a pretty loud signal: You're safe here! Ostensibly, the people present within the multicolored gathering have worked out those cross-race issues already. They are comfortable with cross-cultural relationships, making others feel welcome. People feel a sense of relief because they don't have to think about trying hard to connect with people of other races.

However, I want to add a word of caution: Some make the assumption that because they have many cross-race friendships, their friends have also worked through diversity issues. Not necessarily. Quite a number of people love being in a multiracial setting but have no idea what it takes to create one. They have not taken the time to recognize the five practices that bring people together that I shared in chapter 3:

1. Act neighborly.
2. Share common interests.
3. Be warm and inviting.
4. Offer mutual respect.
5. Respond with kindness.

Having numerous cross-race friends might not relieve you from the obligation of having vulnerable conversations with friends who need to sharpen their interethnic attractiveness, especially those who want to boost their own cross-cultural appeal.

The point is still valid, however, that if you already have a strong base of cross-race friends, this serves as a natural attraction for other cross-race relationships to form in your life. Diversity attracts diversity.

6. Seek mutually rewarding outcomes.

When you meet people whose experiences and ideas satisfy your needs for a friend — and you theirs — the relationship will be mutually rewarding and mutually attractive.

In 2005, I served as a member of the executive committee for the Billy Graham Crusade held in New York City — the last one of his life. I took away thousands of lessons about walking in humility, staying focused on the mission of the gospel, and maintaining Christ-centered living amid pluralism. But one lesson I'll never forget is the unwavering commitment of the Graham organization to include every culture and ethnic group in the planning stages of the crusade. Each month we met, the Asian, African-American, Caucasian, Native American, Latino, and Messianic Jewish communities were all represented in the strategy room. The entire Christian and Catholic traditions were also fully present. This gathering of Christian leaders looked like the ethnic roundtable Professor Justo Gonzalez described in his book *Out of Every Tribe and Nation*.[1]

We all had one desire: for the residents of New York and the surrounding states to hear and receive the gospel. We wanted them to fall in love with Jesus. We walked away full after each planning session. We made new friends across the racial, cultural, and denominational lines.

We all felt closer to the Lord, having earned a once-in-a-lifetime, rewarding opportunity: the pleasure of working with one another and for one of God's generals. The most powerful benefit of living a lifestyle that models diversity, however, is that we can connect in the deepest sense with other Christians despite our racial, cultural, and ethnic differences. Every Christian has a bond with every other Christian that supersedes racial, ethnic, and nationalistic divisions. We have the same spiritual Father, share the same spiritual race and bloodline, and have a common citizenship in heaven. As the apostle Paul declared, "You are no longer foreigners and aliens, but fellow citizens with God's people and members of God's household, built on the foundation of the apostles and prophets, with Christ Jesus himself as the chief cornerstone" (Ephesians 2:19-20). Through the Holy Spirit, the ties to our mutual race, citizenship, and family are eternal and outweigh the ties to our earthly race and citizenship. What more powerful benefit is there?

The yearlong planning session for the crusade taught me more than how to plan to reach a city; I learned to recognize the benefits of connecting with others for the purpose of the gospel.

7. Demonstrate comfort in the friendship.

No amount of dramatic acting ability can mask someone's feeling uncomfortable in cross-cultural situations. There is a clumsiness to his or her interactions, a halting fakeness to the flow of conversation. And, of course, the uneasiness — like the measles — is contagious. The disconnect, even if subtle, is pure and undeniable. No one wants to feel they have to force a relationship to form, grow, and be maintained. That's social torture. People spend time with people who make them feel comfortable.

How can you help others feel comfortable around you? By accepting them without judgment. People can't feel at ease if they feel you're sitting around critiquing them to see if they measure up to some standard of excellence, status, or even success. When you accept others, it is evident in the way you speak to them. Your interaction is not a series of questions aimed at trying to size up which of you is superior to the other. The conversation simply flows, and there is no tension or power play. The conversational playing field is level.

Many cross-race friendships come to a stop because one person keeps making race an issue for no apparent reason. For example, when someone says, "This Puerto Rican guy, who is an accountant, was dating my next-door neighbor." There is no reason for mentioning the guy's Puerto Rican ancestry, so don't. The practice of calling attention to someone's race or ethnicity reveals your unfamiliarity in holding cross-race conversations.

Remember, the nature of healthy cross-race friendships is that each person sees value and gains a specific benefit. If the relationship creates discomfort that outweighs the real or perceived benefits, the relationship will not last. To create a sense of comfort in the relationship, you have to be someone who others find easy to relax around.

If this is your trait, keep taking it easy. If not, don't give up. In the book *Communicating with Strangers*, we learn that our effectiveness in cross-cultural communication can significantly improve if we "are mindful of our communication behavior."[2] In other words, this trait can be developed as you're mindful of its value and importance when speaking cross-culturally.

8. Practice honesty in the relationship.

Trust is built when you are honest in your cross-race relationships, particularly when confrontation occurs. For example, an African-American man told me that once he was hurt by his white friend's culturally insensitive comments that black men on a whole don't prioritize their fathering role in the lives of their children. When the African-American was honest with his friend about how the comment came across and his white friend responded with understanding and an apology, the cross-race friendship was strengthened.

Of all the eight behavioral traits, this particular one is most beneficial to maturing cross-race friendships after they have been formed. As we learned earlier, honesty is a critical ingredient to building trust and credibility. People know where they stand when you are honest with them. Cross-race friendships, like same-race friendships, have their ups and downs. There are more things to tackle in cross-race relationships, however, such as the role of status in the relationship. Therefore, when conflicts or questions arise, honest dialogue must be welcomed.

Honesty is critical in the early stages of the cross-race relationship, and discussion should be couched with words like "I've never had a cross-race friendship before, and if I say something that is offensive, please tell me. I want to learn." Such statements are normal when two people are navigating new social territory.

If you don't want to be that direct, use your skills of observation. People who lack the experience of cross-race friendships can observe how their words are weighed and the type of responses that come back after certain statements are made. Even people skilled in cross-race relationships must be alert in how they are being interpreted so they can make quick adjust-ments along the way. When you make adjustments, you are conveying to the other person, "Your thoughts and opinions matter to me. I'm making the appropriate adjustments so we can both get the maximum benefit from the relationship."

On my oldest daughter's eighteenth birthday, Marlinda and I wanted to surprise her by buying her a dependable used car. After my research, we decided to get a Volkswagen Passat. I searched the Internet for the best deal, which happened to require a ninety-minute drive across the state border. I remem-ber walking into the used-car dealership in Brooklyn, ready to do some fancy negotiations. The owner, a middle-aged man of Middle Eastern descent, politely met me and showed me the Passats he had on his lot. I saw the perfect car for Danielle, and negotiations began.

After a few moments, he mistook for prejudice my insis-tence on a more reasonable price and angrily said to me, "You're talking to me like I'm a terrorist!" I was baffled at his misinterpretation of my haggling for a fair price. Then I put myself in his shoes and thought, *With the rise of national concern with jihadists and Muslim extremists, the decent and law-abiding Middle Easterners like him have had to go on the defensive in order to avoid becoming lumped in with the all-too-common ethnic profile of terrorists.* My simple trip to the car dealership reinforced once again that things can fall apart rather quickly when you are not paying attention to cross-cultural interchanges. I apologized profusely for the misunderstanding, which resulted in our striking a deal at the lower price.

INTERETHNIC APPEAL IS *NOT* TOLERANCE

I need to explain something else that I learned from the focus groups that may surprise you: Tolerance does not make you more racially attractive. Let me explain.

One of the buzzwords in our modern society is *tolerance*. A few years back, there was a series of television commercials designed to promote multiculturalism based on the way they challenged us to become tolerant of the next guy — the guy who's racially or culturally different from us. Tolerance was introduced as the medicine for ailing intercultural relationships.

At face value, tolerance seems like a good thing — a remedy to the ailments of an aversion for diversity. Yet when you investigate the feelings surrounding tolerance, they are not positive, honest, or endemic of an authentic Christ follower. If people tolerate you, it's because they have no choice other than to be connected with you in some way. Being with you is not their first option. It is by default, an obligation; it's forced. The feeling of tolerance undermines the foundation for building healthy cross-race relationships. If you tolerate someone, you don't want to spend time with that person socially. They won't make the invitation list to your party. As Christians, we must build our cross-cultural lives on a stronger, more effective building block than tolerance. Tolerance erodes the essence of dignity and value in each person. Tolerance is not a nice thing.

The idea of *political correctness* (PC) was integrated in the vocabulary and behavioral expectation of mainstream American society in an effort to remedy intolerance. The premise is that a positive code of language and treatment toward others — regardless of their religion, gender, culture, race, or sexual orientation — will mitigate uncomfortable feelings. The code is enforced by the use of certain terms when describing or speaking about others. For example, a deaf person might better respond to the more positive label of *hearing impaired*. If you use PC statements, your intent is clear: You want to make others feel comfortable around you, and you in turn want to feel comfortable around them.

On the surface, the idea behind political correctness seems like a good one. But it's important to note that being politically correct is viewed negatively in most social settings. When someone is practicing political correctness toward you, you likely feel a lack of sincerity from that person. You might feel that the person is patronizing you to get through the awkwardness of the moment.

Real love, on the other hand, emanates from the heart and brings comfort. You must not hesitate to demonstrate genuine love toward other types of people. This attitude communicates that you're willing to break the unspoken social rules to convey love, trust, and respect across cultural lines. Unlike political correctness and tolerance, love cannot be mandated. Love strives for true acceptance of others.

The only solution to combating tolerance is to apply love. Political correctness is not love; it is tolerance. And tolerance is not love. No matter how you slice it, no one wants to be tolerated. Cross-race relationships are built on love and acceptance, period.

CHAPTER 5

TEARING DOWN BARRIERS

Years ago, Phil and his wife, Betty, faithfully attended my church. For the first few months of their membership at Christ Church, they demonstrated genuine excitement and commitment to our vision and ministry. Because the congregation was small at the time, I was able to interact with each family. Phil showed great leadership potential, so I invited him to participate in the church's leadership-development process to sharpen his gifts for greater effectiveness.

As time passed, I noticed that Phil began to resist my efforts to connect with him for mentoring and personal instruction. He wasn't rude, but I was aware of a subtle uneasiness. I thought I had somehow offended Phil and made him uncomfortable.

When I tried to arrange a meeting with him, Phil was evasive. I couldn't get a straight answer from him about a convenient time to meet. Eventually, he began coming up with excuses for missing church services. I noticed that his wife and children came less frequently as well. I couldn't put my finger on what happened, and it bothered me. Sometimes I even thought I might be picking up racial tension between us, as Phil and I weren't of the same race. Other times I thought I had said something to him that he just couldn't forgive or forget. Needless to say, this issue had become the eight-hundred-pound gorilla in the room whenever Phil and his family came to church.

One day I forced a meeting with Phil following a Sunday service. After exchanging pleasantries, I jumped right into my concern, asking Phil if I had offended him in any way. Phil didn't seem surprised because he, too, had apparently noticed the barrier between us. After he told me I hadn't offended him, I tried to discover what the issues were between us. I even broached the topic of race to determine if that was the problem. Each attempt I made was unsuccessful. Phil kept insisting that nothing was wrong and that he was fine in his relationship with me.

Following that afternoon, I put the matter in God's hands and didn't give it any more thought. A few weeks later, Phil and Betty announced their plans to leave the church. They said they would be relocating out of state to live closer to their family. I thanked them for their labor of love at Christ Church and for the fortunate opportunity to have known them. I ended my good-bye with the statement "If there's anything I can do for you guys in the future, please don't hesitate to contact me." And we parted.

About four years later, I received a letter from Phil, saying he would be visiting New Jersey and wanted to get together. After we caught up on each other's lives and families, Phil shocked me by asking me to forgive him for the way he had treated me. Before I could respond, he handed me a letter detailing his apology. I read in silence, grateful to finally have my suspicions about our relationship confirmed. I wasn't crazy after all. From the letter, I learned that the distance between us was rooted in Phil's childhood. His mother constantly rode him about the way he spoke, his manners, and other things that moms try to instill in their children. Her approach was over the top in Phil's case, however.

Phil resisted her heavy-handed methods to get him to speak properly and act in a highly dignified manner. In the letter, Phil wrote,

> Although you were nothing but warm and gracious toward me, I saw in you everything my mother wanted me to be. I'm sure she loved me in her own way, but she never showed it in a way I could understand as a boy. She always insisted that I should be stronger, more articulate – always more. When you suggested leadership-development training, I know now it came from a place of love. But a part of me felt that same inadequacy I felt as a child.

Phil never realized his pent-up anger and resentment toward his mother or knew enough to talk about it until a couple of years after he met me. I embodied the very things he had resisted his whole life, and he projected those ill feelings toward me. The way I spoke and my demeanor were constant reminders of what he rebelled against.

After that incident, Phil and I remained in contact with one another. We still see each other at regional conferences and chat on the phone once a year or so.

TWO KINDS OF BARRIERS

My experience with Phil taught me that barriers should not be ignored and that sometimes we assume there is racial tension when there isn't. A barrier is a wedge that prevents you from connecting socially with someone else. In the context of cross-cultural relationships, a barrier is the social distance we consciously or unconsciously place between us and that other person.

Cross-race barriers come in two forms: those from within and those from without. Both damage any cross-race relationship.

Internal Barriers

We live in a country of roughly 300 million people hailing from thousands of cultures and some two hundred nationalities. Shouldn't it be easy to have tons of cross-race friends? If it isn't, an internal barrier may be standing in your way. Internal barriers, which are a part of your life—your culture, your viewpoint—are difficult to spot because you've lived with them your whole life. Phil had an internal barrier he couldn't see. It took the four years we were apart for him to wrestle through his conflict and finally identify the hurdle.

Behavioral scientist Milton Rokeach unearthed the idea that personal change occurs because of two kinds of stimuli. First, people change when they come into conflict with their own personal values and conscience. Second, people change when social and societal pressure becomes overwhelming and unavoidable.[1] Rokeach was on to something. When a personal crisis arises about your own values and behavior, you are more willing to tackle the internal barriers to cross-race relationships. Your conscience is troubled by your own thoughts of yourself. This was the case with Phil. When he saw that he was disconnected and out of alignment with *his* Christian values, it forced him to identify the barrier and forge a pathway to change.

What does it take for you to feel out of sync with your own values? This is a tough question because no one wakes up one morning and says, *I need to build meaningful cross-race relationships!* without first having a crisis of identity. An internal barrier can be spotted and challenged only when something outside of you troubles your conscience. For instance, you are attracted to the benefits others derive from cross-race friendships and long to be able to laugh, joke, learn from, and socialize with people from other cultures. Your conscience begins to direct you toward the possibility of having a cross-cultural life. If a troubling conscience weren't enough, the Holy Spirit constantly convicts you of your spiritual responsibility to share the love of God with those outside your culture. This can't be done if you are unable or unwilling to cross the great ethnic divide.

As you become increasingly aware of this prompting of the Holy Spirit and the groaning of your conscience, your internal barriers will begin to erode because of the growing disharmony in your personal values. Embracing a lifestyle of diversity is sure to become a greater priority in your life.

External Barriers

Coming from Nigeria to the States on an academic scholarship, Joshua was first indoctrinated into cross-cultural relationships when the white university representative told him during orientation, "Stay away from black Americans. They don't like you guys!" Joshua tearfully told me, "I unknowingly picked up their prejudices and shunned all relationships with black Americans. After graduation, I moved from Washington, D.C., to upstate New York to attend graduate school. I quickly found a church—an all-white congregation—that I would call my home church for the next two years. My Nigerian colleague and I were the only people of color in the church. We were accepted completely. I was unaware that my prejudice toward African-Americans was becoming stronger as I isolated myself due to fear and an unfounded suspicion."

As Joshua discovered, peer pressure can play a significant role in erecting external barriers that get in the way of cross-race relationships. The only way you can resist conforming is when your internal values are deeply justifiable to your own conscience—in other words, when your conscience tells you that your beliefs about a particular issue are right and that society's position is wrong. Joshua was eventually able to overcome the suspicions and isolation toward African-Americans and emerge as an authentic reconciler, but it took exposure and purposeful interaction with African-Americans at work, community outings, and citywide worship events for his suspicions to be dethroned. Most people never address head-on their need to be racially inclusive, but he did. It's possible to intentionally align your personal values with the practice of building healthy cross-race relationships.

FOUR STEPS FOR DEALING WITH CROSS-RACIAL BARRIERS

My incident with Phil gave me the tools to teach others how to tear down their own relational barriers and prompted me to develop this four-step process for dealing with cross-racial barriers:

1. Recognize the barrier.
2. Identify the cause of the barrier.
3. Remove the barrier.
4. Seek outside help if needed.

We can see this four-step process at work in the life of King David as he attempted to rebound after his fall from grace in his sin of adultery with Bathsheba. Because David ignored his sin, it became a barrier in his relationship with God. The Lord sent Nathan the prophet to help David recognize the barrier (see 2 Samuel 12:1-14). Once David became aware of the consequences of his sin, the path was clear to proceed to step 3 in the process: repentance. David cried out to God, "Cleanse me with hyssop, and I will be clean; wash me, and I will be whiter than snow" (Psalm 51:7). He was truly broken up about his need to reconnect with God. Even though David penned the words of this psalm to reflect sorrow for his sin, parts of it show the guilt he had to work through. Verse 3 says, "I know my transgressions, and my sin is always before me."

I suspect that the sins of adultery, betrayal, and murder (of Bathsheba's husband) weighed heavily on David's conscience. Prior to this, he had prided himself in clean living and the practice of the presence of God (see 2 Samuel 6:5; 8:15). Fortunately, Nathan was wise and sensitive enough not to let David wallow in self-pity. Step 4 occurred when Nathan helped David overcome his guilt by saying to him, "The LORD has taken away your sin. You are not going to die" (2 Samuel 12:13).

The barrier to David's intimacy with God was torn down and he was able to freely sing to God, "Restore to me the joy of your salvation and grant me a willing spirit, to sustain me. Then I will teach transgressors your ways, and sinners will turn back to you" (Psalm 51:12-13). Nothing is impossible for God, not even the most difficult relational barriers.

This four-step process can empower you to tear down the

barriers in your life that hinder the development of healthy cross-race relationships. They can also be helpful in stimulating healthy same-race relationships and maturing your relationship with the Lord.

1. Recognize the barrier.

Barriers hinder you from progressing beyond a certain point. They prevent you from taking your relationships beyond the superficial stage to a mutually beneficial dimension. Barriers create a gap between you and the person with whom you're trying to connect. They create emotional disconnects, leaving you aloof and detached. That was the case with Phil. He hid his feelings from me during the early days of our meeting. When I confronted him about the presence of a barrier, he couldn't open up and discuss his emotions honestly.

Remember, one of the top eight ways cross-race relationships form is through honesty in the relationship. You must be honest with yourself if you are going to recognize that a barrier exists in your efforts to form interethnic relationships. If you want to know if you have a barrier in your life toward cross-race relationships, get in a quiet place and ask yourself, *Do I reveal my emotions when I'm around people of other races? Do I respond to their feelings when they share them?* Jot down the thoughts that come to mind.

2. Identify the cause of the barrier.

If you've ever watched a National Basketball Association game on television, you know that the league is primarily made up of African-American players. The complexion of the sport is likely attributable to the huge popularity of basketball in urban communities. In recent years, though, hoop stars are increasingly more diverse, with a large number coming to the NBA from Eastern Europe, Asia, and South America.

After teaching my session "How to Connect Across Racial and Cultural Lines" to some eighty NBA rookies, I was pulled into a room by a program coordinator. Through the interpreter, I learned that a foreign player felt his game had fallen off because of a disconnect between him and his African-American teammates. Throughout the season, the African-American teammates often teased this international player with playful taunts and trash talk, which is common on urban blacktops all across the country. But their humor was lost on him; he did not understand why he was being insulted in this way. He shut down emotionally, and his performance on the basketball court suffered. I was able to help him see that his teammates' words were not intended to be hurtful. I explained that it's common for many within the African-American community to tease one another harmlessly. I told him that African-Americans often tease people they like and that the teasing he was receiving, though rough at times, reflected their fondness of him. When I said this, his face brightened. I later learned that opening up to me was the first time he'd spoken that entire weekend because of his emotional pain. Identifying the cause of the cultural barrier gave this basketball player a new perspective and insight for building cross-race relationships both on and off the court.

Sociologists Larry Samovar and Richard Porter tell us that "anyone who has truly struggled to comprehend another person—even those closest and most like himself—will appreciate the immensity of the challenge of intercultural communication."[2] In Phil's case, it took four years for him to identify the cause of the barrier to our relationship. But, in the case of the ball player, it took only five minutes. Perhaps Phil could have recognized the cause sooner if he had been able to deal with his own pain and bring it to my attention. Tearing down a barrier calls for examining every possible cause.

In both cases, pain got in the way of a cross-cultural connection. When you feel emotionally hurt, pain masks your emotional clarity. Hurt dulls your discernment and clouds your view, giving you a faulty read of a situation and creating a relational barrier. Phil was hurt by his mother's insensitive approach to offering instruction; the NBA player was hurt by the teasing.

The only way to remove the mask of hurt is through forgiveness and repentance, which is the next step in the process. (We'll delve even more deeply into this topic in the next chapter.)

3. Remove the barrier.

Identifying the barrier in a cross-race relationship is one thing, but doing something about it is an entirely different story.

Drawing again from David's memorable act of repentance, we see that he was willing to go to the ends of the earth to build a healthy relationship with God. He desperately wanted the barrier removed. He held himself accountable because his sin had created the disconnect. He wrote, "The sacrifices of God are a broken spirit; a broken and contrite heart, O God, you will not despise" (Psalm 51:17). This kind of contrition and humility is still needed today.

How important is it to you to remove your cross-race barriers? The NBA player had a passionate reason for removing his relational barriers. He wanted to stay in the NBA. Phil had a passionate reason too. He wanted his behavior to align with his Christian faith. Your passionate reason may be that you hate the idea of failing at cross-race relationships. If you really want to remove the barrier to cross-race friendships, your passion will be seen through your dedication, through your unusual intensity and commitment, and by a dogged determination to do so. You will refuse to be a quitter when it comes to removing relational barriers.

Phil's passion for bridge building was evident as I read his letter. I was unaware that he had been determined to discover the reason for our disconnect. But his passion didn't dry up when he found out what had created the barrier. Instead, he wanted to tear it down. To do that, he meditated on our past interactions, searching for the reasons. He also took full responsibility for the condition of our relationship and rendered a decision against himself. Phil's passion to connect with me was clearly demonstrated when he let go of the hurt and asked for my forgiveness.

Phil practiced genuine humility. He did not try to pass the buck or justify, excuse, or rationalize his behavior. He was the culprit and he owned it — totally. The NBA player also showed humility when he asked for my input about his dilemma. His humility required a number of steps. First, he had to explain his problem to his interpreter, who in turn had to tell it to the player's representative. The player representative had to request that I meet with the rookie, which called for his sharing the problem with me. Once we were in the private room, the player had to retell his personal problem all over again through his interpreter. It took a tremendous amount of humility on his part to share this social challenge with me, a total stranger. You can't avoid paying the price of humility. It's the evidence of your passion to remove the barrier to forming cross-race relationships.

In most cases, passion spurs resourcefulness. Phil knew that a phone call could set the stage for a meeting. But because he wanted to ensure that his request for forgiveness was communicated effectively, he put all that information in a letter. Writers are more precise than speakers. Anne Lamott, author of the award-winning book *Bird by Bird*, conveyed, "When writers make us shake our heads with the exactness of their prose and their truths, and even make us laugh about ourselves or life, our buoyancy is restored."[3] Phil's well-crafted letter restored my buoyancy in pursuing a healthy relationship with him.

4. Seek outside help if needed.

The NBA rookie knew that his barrier could be removed only with the help of others. He did not know what was causing the barrier, but he knew he needed to tear it down. He seized the moment and requested a private meeting with me.

There is no crime in requesting help. At times, a person-to-person interaction is needed. I recommend that you seek out a coach if you feel stuck. They are all around, although they might not be wearing a label marked "Cross-Cultural Coach." A coach is anyone with at least a little more experience than you in the area in which you're seeking to grow. This could be a fellow church member or a coworker; anyone with more cross-cultural experience than you would be of great benefit. Your coach will help you locate your barrier, identify what caused it, and help you identify ways to overcome it. If a barrier is preventing you from developing cross-race relationships, make a commitment to get the help you need.

BE AN ADVOCATE

Some people don't need a coach; they need an advocate. An advocate is a compassionate person who feels your pain and does something about it. Advocates assist others in removing their barriers so that becoming a reconciler is possible. In her 1982 address at Harvard's Class Day Exercises, Mother Teresa said, "[Some people are] hungry not only for bread—but hungry for love. . . . Naked not only for clothing—but naked for human dignity and respect. . . . Homeless not only for want of a room of bricks—but homeless because of rejection."[4] The advocate's job is to either provide the solution or to help connect the needy person with someone who has the solution.

Several years ago, I started asking people about their journeys into lifestyles of diversity. I remember sitting down with Aashil, a young information technology consultant who had a quiet personality. Aashil is about twenty-one years old and of Indian descent. His bronze-colored skin made him appear almost Middle Eastern in his complexion, which, he noted, was the target of a lot of pain during high school.

Aashil said, "I was the only Indian in my class. Although I was born here in the United States, my parents and I migrated back to India for about a decade when I was a child. Upon my return as a teenager, I began to deal with cross-cultural issues in high school. I was shunned and labeled by the other students as an unsafe person. In the wake of September 11th and heightened fears of terrorists, the naïve students lumped me into this profile because of the color of my skin."

Aashil spoke with his professor about what was happening, and the wise teacher confronted the other students and put an end to their culturally insensitive behavior. The teacher challenged the class not to erect barriers that isolate cultures from one another and warned how isolation creates suspicion that ends in prejudice. He explained to the students that both parties can become prejudiced because of isolation from one another.

Elated by this vindication by a white teacher, Aashil found it easy to tear down the barriers that he had erected in his heart. He said, "Pastor, that was the first time someone had become an advocate on my behalf. The teacher understood my concerns, and through his talking with the class, my painful silence was heard loudly by everyone."

I immediately recognized that the teacher's advocacy prevented Aashil from walking down the road of self-hatred or even prejudice. There are many Aashils in our social circles— people who are untouched by reconciliation because the advocates have remained silent. Biblical advocacy demands that we stand up for the weak, the oppressed, and the marginalized in our society, whose voices go unheard. I want to challenge you to stand up for the Aashils in your life by first breaking through your own barriers to cross-race friendships.

CHAPTER 6

THE POWER OF FORGIVENESS

I prayed fervently for the wisdom to get my congregation to connect with my lesson called "Building Healthy Cross-Race Relationships." I wanted them to understand that embracing this teaching was more than a nice gesture; it was an important step in strengthening their relationship with God.

After a couple of days of praying, an idea came to me as I was reading about Jesus washing the disciples' feet (see John 13). As the story goes, Jesus got up from the evening meal, wrapped a towel around His waist, washed His disciples' feet, and dried them with the towel. Peter, the infamously outspoken disciple, objected by telling Jesus, "No, . . . you shall never wash my feet" (verse 8). For Peter, the idea of Jesus washing his feet was inconceivable. First, foot washing was a menial task performed by servants. In fact, the renowned New Testament Greek scholar Leon Morris pointed out that "[foot washing] was so menial that a Hebrew slave was not required to perform it, though a Gentile slave might be."[1] Second, Jesus was *his* Master, not the other way around. Jesus responded to Peter's objection, saying, "Unless I wash you, you have no part with me," so Peter gave in.

Jesus was teaching the disciples a tremendous lesson: Serving someone else is a powerful display of love. Hearts become vulnerable during a foot-washing ceremony. The Scripture says, "The evening meal was being served, and the devil had already prompted Judas Iscariot, son of Simon, to betray Jesus" (John 13:2). Jesus gave Judas one last opportunity to come clean and get free from his scheme to give Him up for thirty pieces of silver. He said, "A person who has had a bath needs only to wash his feet; his whole body is clean. And you are clean, though not every one of you" (verses 10-11). Cold-blooded Judas managed to keep a dirty heart while having clean feet. He could not find room within his soul to ask for forgiveness of the sin of disloyalty and betrayal. Even though Judas did not respond to Jesus' foot washing with tears of repentance and confession, the act was still an undeniable symbol of humility and forgiveness, especially from a standpoint of social superiority.

After reading the story again, I was sold. The humble act of foot washing is still a potent spiritual exercise that can yield a clean heart. Regardless of whether a person is the victimizer or the victim of a prejudiced act, foot washing can be a therapeutic practice if the Holy Spirit is involved. I decided to have two men—one white, the other black—wash each other's feet publicly to demonstrate forgiveness of the historic racial problems stemming from their forefathers.

I wanted the foot washing to set the stage for the congregation to open their hearts to almighty God, who knew how to clean sin-stained hearts of racism. The act had to be presented as more than a historical occasion with Jesus and

His disciples; it had to be positioned as a medicinal act that unites with our faith to bring us to a place of freedom.

That Sunday morning, I was prepared with basin, towel, and a pitcher of water. Scott, an African-American man, agreed to participate in this important teaching moment. I knew that he had struggled with cross-race friendships because of the destructive role racism played in his own family, so I asked him to share his story during the actual foot washing. His counterpart that morning was Ron, a white brother who grew up with a stronghold of prejudice toward blacks. Only when he came to know Jesus as his Savior was his heart softened and accepting of blacks.

I instructed both men privately, "Guys, the goal of my sermon is to create a moment for hearts to be opened to accepting people of different races. This change of heart can come only when forgiveness is extended and received." I said that forgiveness must be extended with honesty and full ownership of the wrongdoing in order for its healing power to be released. Similarly, forgiveness must be embraced so that its curative effects can take root in the heart of the wounded person.

Then I laid out my plan to the two men: "I will explain to the congregation what foot washing means and then give each of you an opportunity to speak directly to the other as the representative for your race. For example, as Ron is seated facing you, Scott, and as you wash his feet, share with him how the prejudice from the white race has impacted you. But, when you finish, in your own words ask for his forgiveness for harboring ill will and anger toward him and members of his race."

We discussed how after Scott washed and dried Ron's feet, the two would change places and go through the process again. This time Ron would wash Scott's feet while sharing his struggles and his need for forgiveness. Once the plan was clear, we walked into the sanctuary armed with a God-given illustration that had the potential to free a lot of people from the baggage of prejudice.

As Scott washed Ron's feet, he choked up. He revealed that years of racial victimization had led his father to abuse alcohol. He had been mistreated by whites solely on the basis of his skin color. Scott spoke about his anger toward whites and his need to remove the barrier that prevented him from connecting with whites the way he knew that God wanted him to. His tears fell into the basin, mixing with the water used to wash Ron's feet. Scott's heartfelt plea for forgiveness echoed throughout the sanctuary. Because Ron was acting as a representative of the white race, his forgiveness was critical for Scott's healing. Without hesitation, Ron forgave Scott. A palpable ripple effect swept across the sanctuary as other African-Americans allowed their racially torn hearts to be washed by Ron's all-important words of forgiveness.

After we composed ourselves, the two men switched places. This time Scott sat in the chair and Ron wrapped the towel around his waist and held the pitcher of water in his hands. As he poured water over Scott's feet, I could sense that Ron's heart was being emptied of all the prejudiced feelings of superiority toward other races. Ron shared his childhood experiences of growing up with ideas of white supremacy. He admitted that he'd embraced that philosophy and behaved accordingly throughout his life. But on this day he said, "Can you forgive me for thinking, acting, and treating you as lesser than me? I realize that I need your forgiveness to be the man I want to be. Will you free me today?"

This was a holy moment. Forgiveness and repentance were gifts wrapped up and handed to us that morning. This moment is what J. Oswald Chambers meant when he wrote in *My Utmost for His Highest*,

> The bedrock of Christianity is repentance. Strictly speaking, a man cannot repent when he chooses; repentance is a gift of God. The old Puritans used to pray for "the gift of tears." If ever you cease to know the virtue of repentance, you are in darkness. Examine yourself and see if you have forgotten how to be sorry.[2]

That Sunday morning, the entire congregation received the gift of tears as the power of forgiveness washed over their hearts. When the words "I forgive you" left Scott's lips, he freed Ron and every member of the white race who sat there in need of forgiveness from the enslavement of prejudice. At that moment, the Holy Spirit took over the service, and it was no longer under my pastoral leadership. He was now in full control and I was a silent observer. I watched. I wept. I, too, was healed.

UNDERSTANDING THE VALUE OF FORGIVENESS

The study of interpersonal forgiveness is a relatively new trend in academic circles. It is being researched at a surprising pace, however. In May 1998, the John Templeton Foundation awarded research grants for the study of forgiveness to twenty-nine scholars. Former president Jimmy Carter, Archbishop Desmond Tutu, and former missionary Elisabeth Elliot are leading a ten-million-dollar "Campaign for Forgiveness Research." Further, social scientists are catching up with the religious community, recognizing that forgiveness helps victims of prejudice and injustice by rebuilding their sense of value. Forgiveness contains lots of power.

A number of leaders passionately said at the 2001 World Conference Against Racism that Western powers should apologize for four hundred years of slavery. Nigerian president Olusegun Obasanjo pointed out on the second day of the eight-day conference, "We must demonstrate the political will and assume the responsibility for the historical wrongs that are owed to the victims of slavery, that an apology be extended by states which actively practiced and benefited themselves from slavery."[3] As you probably know, Nigeria was a former British colony. Joschka Fischer, formerly Germany's foreign minister, responded, saying that recognition of guilt was the way to restore to the victims and their descendants "the dignity of which they were robbed." He then went on to say, "I should therefore like to do that here and now on behalf of the Federal Republic of Germany."[4]

Forgiveness can take place on national, regional, local, and personal levels. This gift is valuable only when it's given away. In June 1998, hundreds of people in Tulsa, Oklahoma—both black and white—gathered for what would be an emotional assembly of repentance. The location was an empty lot that was once home to a thriving African-American business district—that is, until it was decimated by the events of June 21, 1921, when one of the worst race riots in our nation's history began after an angry mob called for the lynching of a black man accused of attacking a white elevator operator. Some three hundred people were killed and the Greenwood district lay in ruins.

On the anniversary, white ministers led the whites in the crowd to humbly ask the African-Americans to forgive them for the acts of racial injustice by their white forefathers. African-American ministers then led the blacks in pardoning the whites. Asking for and receiving forgiveness were both necessary to break down the barriers of cross-race friendships. In the audience that Monday was Mabel Little, a 101-year-old survivor of the riots. It was reported that she said of this assembly of repentance, "I'm the happiest person in the world, today."[5]

MAKING CROSS-RACE FORGIVENESS PERSONAL

As children, we learned to apologize when we hurt someone on the playground, even when we hurt them inadvertently. I love to see the way kids are able to return to their play after asking one another for forgiveness. Their relationship appears undamaged and solid, just as if the infraction never occurred. How innocent. How pure. How beautiful. The power of this simple, uncomplicated action should never be underestimated. Saying "I'm sorry" has the power to soften the human heart and to right wrongs, even those historic societal ills that have resulted in wide racial divisions. Forgiveness is an indispensible part of learning how to be a reconciler.

Forgiveness means to set free, pardon, and let go. The nineteenth-century preacher E. H. Chapin said, "Never does the human soul appear so strong as when it forgoes revenge and dares to forgive an injury."[6] And Jesus taught us that forgiveness carries healing powers. It can heal the most broken-hearted or abused soul. Sometimes forgiveness is the antidote that heals when traditional medicine fails. This was the case when Christ declared to the paralyzed man, "Friend, your sins are forgiven" (Luke 5:20). After hearing this, the man immediately got up from his mat and walked.

The power to forgive is not just at Jesus' disposal; we, too, can forgive. He said, "Whatever you ask for in prayer, believe that you have received it, and it will be yours. And when you stand praying, if you hold anything against anyone, forgive him, so that your Father in heaven may forgive you your sins" (Mark 11:24-25). I believe in the omnipotence of God. Indeed, He is all-powerful, yet Jesus taught that God's power is limited by hardened hearts. That's why it's so important to obey the law of God, which says to forgive those who've hurt you so that you can fully access all of God's promises and blessings (see Ephesians 4:31-32). Forgiveness releases the power of God. Resentment, or unforgiveness, restrains it.

Forgiveness bridges the divide by removing the barriers between us and members of other races — barriers that may have been erected through our suspicions or painful cross-racial experiences. If you are to foster cross-race relationships, you must forgive people from other races. And the person with whom you are seeking to build a friendship will also have to forgive. Forgiveness must flow from both parties in order for healing to occur and cross-race friendships to be formed.

Some people are not aware of their need to seek forgiveness, even though their social circles are largely monoracial. Alex, a Taiwanese immigrant to the United States, had to learn to process his prejudices when his American-born daughters started befriending people of different races. Alex verbalized his natural reactions to his girls: "We Chinese have thousands of years of civilized history under our belts. Those people can't teach us anything or bring any value to our lives." To his surprise, his daughters passionately corrected him by saying, "They are people too. You must respect them." Slowly, Alex began to change, and his Christian witness grew to become more in keeping with the Bible. The Scripture is right in that "a little child will lead them" (Isaiah 11:6).

Had he not been confronted by his daughters' words, Alex would not have realized how he had rationalized away his prejudices. Many people unknowingly do the same. When the topic of forgiveness is broached in the arena of cross-race relationships, those people seldom notice how it applies to them. And the Holy Spirit must bring it to light to draw out our need for forgiveness. Fortunately, for Alex, the Holy Spirit used his daughters to help him see the light. Now Alex enjoys his status as a cross-cultural ambassador for Christ.

Your personal healing can be delayed or prevented if, because of prejudice, you manipulate, induce guilt, or attempt to exert control over the "offending race or individual" by withholding forgiveness. As a result, resentment festers in the offender, true repentance is blocked, and love toward the wronged party is stifled.

Do you remember Jim Henson, the creator of the Muppets? He died suddenly in 1990. He was very sick, but he assumed his flu-like symptoms were just that—the flu. Truth was he had bacterial pneumonia, a serious but treatable condition. Henson had no idea how sick he really was. In the same way, scores of people reason that they're just fine in the way they view other races. Because they basically have goodwill toward people of other races, they believe they're okay and reason that it's a mild case of racial discomfort when, in fact, it's more serious than that. Just as Jim Henson did not recognize the seriousness of his illness, these people don't realize that they're suffering from a larger issue of sinfulness within their racially torn hearts. They tell themselves, *I'm polite to everybody no matter what color they are. I'm pretty good, especially when I consider all the bigots in society.* But these thoughts and statements are meaningless if forgiveness isn't applied to bridge the divide between us and members of other races. If you are to develop cross-race relationships, you must forgive people from other races for the issues that make you keep them at a distance.

Coming from Ghana, Atu never experienced racial prejudice until he came to the States. The pain of being devalued as a man to a lower status than his white colleagues, despite the fact that he held a master's degree in information technology versus their two-year associate's degrees, became a major sticking point in his cross-cultural journey. When I asked him about his cross-cultural experiences, Atu tearfully confessed, [The devaluing of my status] affected my thinking and the way I looked at myself. It was not until this Polish lady — a coworker — befriended me through a common hobby we both held that I began the journey of forgiveness. My healing began when she curiously read some of my personal poetry, which was lying on my desk. She liked it and encouraged me to keep writing. This white lady saw value in me, a black man. Her encouragement enabled me to slowly drop my emotional guards and embrace Christ's call to live beyond the limits of my own culture.

"We would meet for lunch and talk about poetry. Over time our conversation expanded beyond the subject of poetry to the topic of Christianity, my religion. As God would have it, I was able to lead her to faith in Christ. Looking back, we were both being used by God. I was used to lead her to Christ, and she was used to lead me into the world of diversity. I also learned that I cannot lump all whites into the same category in the same way that I can't lump all blacks or all Asians or whomever into any single category of contempt."

WHAT FORGIVENESS IS NOT

The road to forgiveness is often blocked by faulty notions that trip us up along the way from pain to peace. Many people have been derailed by these misconceptions and have aborted the journey altogether. Let's clarify what forgiveness is not in order to correct some common misunderstandings about it.

Forgiveness does not mean superficial pardon.

True exoneration cuts deep. In fact, it is most effective when coupled with accountability. In 1987, Jose Morales was wrongly charged and imprisoned for murder. The real killer, Jesus Fornes, admitted guilt to Father Towle, a Catholic priest: "He [Fornes] was suffering deeply inside himself. He came to me, not in a confessional situation but as a friend," Towle recalled. "I did bless him at the end of our conversation. I said to him, 'Do you want the forgiveness of God?' He said, 'Yes.' I said, 'You have to ask for it.' I gave him absolution and said, 'Now go to the court and tell them everything that you've told me.' And that is exactly what he did. He made a public declaration of everything he'd said to me."[7]

As it turns out, Fornes never served jail time. His lawyer told him to keep quiet about his crime. That type of confession and request for forgiveness is what I call "detached forgiveness." Fornes eased his conscience by getting a priest to bless him, yet when faced with imprisonment, he chose to hide behind a legal loophole, detaching himself from the injustice he had caused Jose Morales, the guy who got the bum rap. Ten years later, Fornes died and the priest and public defender came forward and shared evidence of Fornes' guilt. Shortly afterward, Morales was released from jail after serving thirteen years for a crime he did not commit. To be sure, Morales suffered a great deal. We could debate the ethics of Father Towle, who withheld information that kept the wrong man imprisoned. Honesty and growth are produced only when you accept the penalty for the wrong you committed.

Forgiveness does not excuse the guilty party.

Studies at UCLA in 2008 showed that "fairness is activating the same part of the brain that responds to food in rats. . . . This is consistent with the notion that being treated fairly satisfies a basic need."[8]

Extending forgiveness is acknowledging the moral side of the infraction. When you offer forgiveness, you let go of any resentment you hold toward the offender. Forgiveness also recognizes that prejudice had devalued the other person. Forgiveness restores their dignity. However, forgiveness does not excuse the guilty party from paying for the crime. For instance, if I stole your car and later expressed sorrow, the apology—though important—would not make you whole. Not only do I have to return your car, I have to pay for all damages my wrongdoing has caused you. In some instances, money will pay only partially for the crime. Imprisonment will be the other portion of the payment.

Don't confuse forgiveness with justice or the elimination of justice. They are two separate issues.

Forgiveness does not guarantee reconciliation.

Khadijah, an African-American woman, was part of a high school gospel choir at the local Catholic school. To her surprise, one day her vigorous clapping to the rhythmic music landed her in the principal's office. She was told, "We don't clap like that in Catholic school." Khadijah left the office thinking, *You feel something negative about my culture and now you're imposing it on me.* She admitted to me, "Pastor, I started a ten-year journey and conscious sense of prejudice — prejudice against me. I no longer viewed myself first as a woman. I now saw myself as others saw me: Black was first and being a woman was second. Although I was able to formulate some cross-cultural relationships, I was always guarded and on the defense for any possible racial slurs or cultural jabs."

Khadijah unconsciously discovered that forgiveness and reconciliation are two separate and distinct acts. She had forgiven her principal but still kept an emotional distance from other whites.

Prejudice is inherently painful. You can forgive someone, which will provide you with a platform and a process for racial reconciliation, but you still have to intentionally seek to be reconciled to that person. To achieve reconciliation, you have to address the pain of the past. Reconciliation also requires a social connection. Meaningful cross-race relationships cannot be built abstractly but must be created in the practical and social sides of life.

Forgiveness does not mean the elimination of healthy boundaries.

Some think forgiveness means erasing the boundaries that safeguard your life and your heart. Not so! A boundary is a way of saying, *I am a human being with the right to be respected.* In the case of a verbally abusive spouse, forgiveness may be requested after a barrage of painful words has been spoken. As an act of graciousness, you may willingly forgive your spouse, but you have a moral responsibility to safeguard your dignity. This occurs when you say to your spouse, "I will not allow you to speak to me that way again. It's wrong and it will not be tolerated."

Because you value your dignity, you must maintain healthy boundaries. In a professional setting, you can say to the offending party, perhaps a colleague, "It is unacceptable for you to make racial slurs or derogatory jokes around me. I will not accept it. If it happens again, I will initiate a discriminatory action complaint through our human resources department and with my attorney."

Don't allow the journey of forgiveness to be impeded in your life because of the common misunderstanding of forgiveness and healthy boundaries. They are separate issues and should always be viewed as such.

Let me show you a process I've used over the years to help others practice forgiveness.

PRACTICING FORGIVENESS

Forgiveness is a four-step process. First, the wronged party must hold the individual or group who caused the injury accountable. Second, forgiveness is acknowledging that the person or group who caused the injury is fallible, flawed, and complicated. Third, the wronged party surrenders the urge to get even. Fourth, the forgiver must shift his or her thinking toward the repentant party from negative to positive.

1. Hold someone accountable for the hurt.

How can forgiveness occur if no one is at fault? Forgiveness requires that blame be levied against the person who injured you. You can only forgive people you hold responsible. Blame means that you have processed the emotional or physical wrongdoing and that every indicator points to the culpability of a certain party.

This is what Scott and Ron did when using the other as the representative of his particular race. This is what the Nigerian president did in the 2001 World Conference Against Racism and what the German foreign minister did when he accepted the blame of past racism. Holding someone accountable is an important step in the forgiveness and healing process.

2. Acknowledge that people are flawed and fallible.

The second step in the journey of forgiveness is to acknowledge that individuals, clans, and even entire governments are flawed and fallible in their treatment and judgments of others. Shortly after Megawati Sukarnoputri became president of Indonesia in 2001, one of her first duties in the area of human rights was to acknowledge that previous governments had made many mistakes. She said, "For that, personally and on behalf of the government as the president of Indonesia, I offer my deep apologies to the people of Aceh."[9]

The Aceh people are a blend of many races but are usually taller and fairer in complexion than most other Indonesians. President Sukarnoputri went on to admit that the people of Aceh had suffered largely due to inappropriate national policies.[10] This public acknowledgment weighed heavily toward the healing process. The individuals who were wronged historically by the government and the people in the majority now felt that the injustices were acknowledged and owned. This also communicated that members of the government were needy, complicated, and flawed people. Whether you are the one extending forgiveness or receiving it, you must admit that you also are flawed, complicated, needy, and susceptible of making grave mistakes that result in the harm and mistreatment of others.

3. Surrender your need to get even.

You cannot fully forgive someone if you're busy plotting revenge. This mindset is morally and philosophically impractical. To forgive, you must surrender your urge to get even. Surrendering is simply another way of saying that two wrongs don't make a right. This step in the healing journey occurs when you say to yourself or another — perhaps a representative of the group who historically hurt you or your forefathers — "I give up my need to get even with you."

4. Change your attitude toward the offender.

Forgiveness moves us away from pain and toward wholeness. Forgiveness is also a gift you give yourself. It releases you from a self-imposed prison of past hurts. Living in unforgiveness shackles you to yesterday's pain and erects barriers to forming friendships. Forgiveness frees you from the negative feelings you hold toward your offender and allows you to grow. It enables you to connect and live a full and complete life, enjoying relationships with every race, ethnic, and cultural group.

CHOOSE FORGIVENESS

Stanley Hauerwas, author of *The Peaceable Kingdom*, states that we fear accepting forgiveness from another because such a gift makes us powerless and we fear the loss of control.[11] When we grant forgiveness, we cede control of our destiny to God, who is the Creator and ultimate giver of forgiveness. But only when we accept His forgiveness and the forgiveness of others can we offer forgiveness and bridge the racial divide.

Is forgiveness from racial pain humanly possible? The answer is a resounding yes! Without forgiveness, prejudice wins. Go ahead! Choose forgiveness and find healing and wholeness.

Take a few minutes right now to find a quiet, private place where you can offer a brief prayer to God. It might go like this:

> Dear God, my heart has been filled with pain and anger toward other races because of how I and my forefathers have been treated. I realize that the offenders were flawed and had damaging practices. I don't want revenge; I want healing. So today, here and now, I ask You to forgive me for what I've allowed to live in my heart. Set me free! Help me cross cultures easily and build meaningful cross-race friendships that will bless the lives of many people. I ask You these things in the name of Your dear Son, Jesus Christ. Amen.

Congratulations! You've allowed the power of forgiveness to break the barriers to forming cross-race relationships in your life.

CHAPTER 7

TURNING THEORY INTO PRACTICE

How do you turn dreams into reality? The answer is the same for the development of cross-cultural talent as it is for the acquisition of athletic skills such as swimming. Michael Phelps won eight gold medals in the swimming competition at the Beijing 2008 Olympics. His dream was always to be an Olympian. He knew one thing: The theory and dream of winning a medal—especially the gold medal—comes about only through lots of practice.

His training regimen was very demanding. He practiced eleven or twelve times per week. He swam at least once every day (including Sunday), and four or five times a week he added a second daily practice. He swam about fifty miles each day. His preparation went beyond the pool. It also entailed a proper diet. He ate twelve thousand calories per day just to keep his weight up from the workouts. His typical breakfast was three fried-egg sandwiches, with cheese, tomatoes, lettuce, fried onions, and mayonnaise, followed by three chocolate chip pancakes, a five-egg omelet, three sugar-coated slices of French toast, and a bowl of grits (a maize-based porridge), washed down with two cups of coffee.[1] Phelps did all this for years in an effort to compete in the Olympics. But he wanted more than to simply swim well; he wanted the gold.

If you have been working your way through this book, you have been getting ready to win at the challenge of forming strong cross-race relationships. And if you've been stuck at this spot for years, it's time to make a shift. Even the USS *Intrepid*—a sixty-four-year-old World War II ship at port in the same spot for twenty-four years—was able to be moved. In the first attempt on November 6, 2006, the 36,000-ton carrier moved only a few feet before the propellers dug into the bottom, the tide dropped, and the mission was scrubbed. However, on Tuesday, December 6, 2006, after three weeks of dredging, nearly 40,000 cubic yards of muck was removed from under the ship and around its four giant screws. The ship was freed so that it could make a smooth departure to a more permanent home.[2]

If a 36,000-ton carrier can be moved from the same spot where it was stuck in the mud, you can move into a racially diverse pool of friends. It's time to deliver. No more excuses. The key is making up your mind to turn theory—the study of diversity—into the intentional practice of reconciliation. Others have successfully done it, and so can you.

The way to turn theory into practice is to face potential risks with courage.

BE WILLING TO TAKE RISKS

It takes courage to face the possibility of rejection when you extend your hand of friendship across the racial divide.

When a local Presbyterian church placed Pastor Stephanie, a white woman who had recently graduated from seminary, into a predominantly Chinese congregation, the cultural sparks began to fly. The congregation felt misunderstood, and she felt rejected. The cultural divide quickly widened as the church resisted all of the pastor's attempts to improve the ministry of the church. The congregation felt that their new pastor lacked the ability to minister to them because she wasn't Chinese and knew nothing about their culture. In danger of failing at her first ministry assignment, Pastor Stephanie needed to act swiftly. To avoid further cultural disconnection, she asked one of the leading families in the church to mentor her on Chinese culture. Her idea was to learn some Bible verses in Mandarin and become more adept in Chinese culture.

As Huang Fu, the man who opened his home to Pastor Stephanie, recounted the story to me, he shared how he and the pastor met weekly for tea and lessons about Chinese culture. There were many comical moments stemming from her attempt to learn to speak some in Chinese, but these only served to endear her to the congregation. For example, Pastor Stephanie tried to end some of her sermons in Mandarin. One time she placed the guttural sounds in the wrong place in her pronunciation. As she preached on the account of Jesus' raising Lazarus from the dead, her mispronunciation and wrong placement of emphasis in the words ended up with Jesus' telling Lazarus, "Don't come out from the grave! Stay there!" The congregation laughed in such a hearty way that the sermon became a huge success. Huang Fu said, "I was able to see with my own eyes and experience a modern-day miracle. God used the language blunders of a white American female pastor to knit her heart with our Asian congregation." Indeed, "God chose the foolish things of the world to shame the wise" (1 Corinthians 1:27).

Pastor Stephanie effectively served that congregation for a number of years before she moved to California as part of her husband's job relocation. "Before she left, it was obvious to everyone, including me, that we could become a cross-cultural community despite the role our strong Asian culture played in our daily lives," Huang Fu said.

Like Pastor Stephanie, you may make a few blunders when attempting to form cross-race friendships, but the rewards far outweigh the mistakes. If you are taking risks to develop cross-race friendships, it means you're committed to growing as a reconciler.

That's exactly what I told Frances when her company hired me as a cross-cultural consultant to advance their ongoing development. Frances was a newly hired division manager responsible for overseeing an area of the organization with approximately two hundred employees and volunteers. She was a young, bright, and energetic leader, ready to tackle large and small problems without hesitation. Frances had a major blind spot, though: She was unable to connect with and effectively engage the people within her department who were racially different from her.

As I talked with people who represented a cross-section of races within the organization, I learned that Frances was not prejudiced; she was just unschooled in the realm of cross-race relationships. Her Caribbean heritage had not afforded her the cross-cultural experience needed to thrive in her new position. This is not the case with all Caribbean people, but it was with Frances. She placed other races above her own in terms of perceived value and behaved as if she was intimidated by them.

Her fear caused her to pull away from other races, professionally and relationally.

Frances' problem was affecting the organization's value of diversity. Equal opportunity for advancement was becoming impossible for all races within her division because she was unconsciously favoring members of her own race by giving them the key assignments and providing them with critical input. My solution to her problem, which she embraced, was for her to take the courageous step of connecting with one person of a different race over the following week. I instructed her to instinctively trust this person based on how she'd seen him or her deal with others. Frances was to strike up a conversation, divulging that she became nervous when speaking to a white person. She was to admit to the person that she was raised on an island where she perceived white people as more valuable than blacks. Although she knew that was incorrect, she was still stuck behind the faulty perception.

It took a lot of courage, but Frances had this conversation with one of her coworkers. To her surprise, she was received with open arms. Her coworker didn't ridicule or belittle her for struggling with those earlier thoughts. Over the next several months, she made steady progress. She began sitting with nonblacks during lunch breaks to build a social connection. She even bought a few books on multiculturalism to understand the different styles of communication needed to develop cross-race friendships. Frances realized that her personal development hinged on taking emotional risks. These risks were directly associated with being intentional about making changes that would result in her cross-cultural growth.

INTENTIONAL OR UNINTENTIONAL?

While Frances built interracial friendships by being intentional, some people enjoy cross-cultural relationships that form by happenstance. Rather than planning to meet someone of another race, they form these friendships effortlessly. Don't write this off as impossible. It very well may happen that way for you. You're ready for such an experience if you've worked out certain issues of the heart, such as placing everyone on the same social status and removing ethnic barriers through the power of forgiveness. It may surprise you how significantly these changes can position you for real-life experiences that wouldn't have otherwise occurred.

Chris, a white pastor, was running errands for his family one Saturday afternoon when he noticed a new church building going up. It was almost completed and it looked magnificent. He had to stop to take a closer look because, apart from its beauty, the building was quite large. *I'd love to meet the pastor who could build such a large church in these hard economic times*, he thought. Chris got his wish. As he got out of the car and walked around the almost-completed building, a tall African-American man walked out of the partially completed lobby. "How may I help you?" he asked. "I'm the pastor of this church." Chris introduced himself as a pastor in the community and shared his admiration of the new worship space.

The two men struck up a conversation and, although they were of different races and denominations, found a natural bridge to build a relationship. Chris promised to attend the building's dedication ceremony, which was scheduled to occur approximately two months later. They exchanged information and, sure enough, when the dedication service was held, Chris was present. From that accidental meeting on a Saturday morning, the two men, who had never enjoyed a meaningful cross-race relationship before, began to build a growing friendship that was mutually rewarding. They swapped evangelistic methods and strategies and even held worship services together in an attempt to create a stronger cross-cultural experience for their congregations. When Chris shared this story with me, I knew that it occurred only because he was courageously willing to attempt to build a meaningful cross-race friendship.

When your heart is settled on building cross-cultural relationships and you no longer vacillate about its importance in your life, everything about you—your facial expressions, unconscious behavior, and body language—echo your heart's desire to walk in diversity. When the confusion of how cross-race relationships are formed is laid to rest, you naturally become more racially attractive.

On the other hand, if you have to be more intentional about attracting cross-race friends, that's great too. If you're wired to be more pragmatic and cerebral, cross-race relationships will emerge based on your planning and positioning yourself to achieve this goal. One style is not better than the other. Whether your cross-race friendship forms intentionally or unintentionally doesn't matter. The goal is to enjoy the benefits associated with such relationships.

DIFFERENT TIMES CALL FOR DIFFERENT STRATEGIES

Don't limit your focus to simply forming a cross-race relationship; make it your goal for those friendships to be healthy and strong. This point is particularly important because some social theorists claim that the goal in cross-race relationships is to settle for weak, superficial bonds.

Mark Granovetter, a sociologist at Stanford University, created a theory on intergroup relations. The theory, developed in the wake of the civil rights movement, claims that in the case of cross-race relationships, weak ties, which take less time to develop than strong ties, may be more of a realistic expectation since there is a natural preference for same-race relationships over that of cross-race ones.[3] I agree partially with this point, but I cannot settle for it as *the* goal we are to aim for. The following stories will show you why.

Todd, an African-American man, always enjoyed an effortless lifestyle of making friends across racial and cultural lines. His whole life spoke of diversity. The only challenges Todd recalls in the arena of cross-race friendships were the ones that surfaced as a result of his courtship and marriage to a white woman named Betty. When they first started dating, they were students at a popular evangelical Christian college. Todd had two white roommates at the time, Peter and Brian, who were good friends, or so he thought.

He told me, "We met each other at the college and became friends because we were all interested in music. The three of us played in a traveling band sponsored by the school. But they immediately turned against me when I started dating Betty. I later discovered that they had a big problem with interracial dating. Their perspective of cross-race friendships did not include interracial romance. They never told me this directly, but they talked with other people about it behind my back. They even tried to turn Betty against me by speaking negatively about me to her. This was especially hurtful because prior to this, these guys were my close friends—the kind of friends who held no secrets from one another. We never even had to talk about matters of race or culture because the three of us gelled so well.

"When I confronted them about their gossip, Peter apologized and we were able to reconcile, although the relationship was never quite the same again. Brian, on the other hand, was never honest about his prejudicial feelings and actions. I learned from that experience that a cross-race experience cannot be strong and healthy if it's held together by weak ties. After graduating, Betty and I got married, and we've enjoyed a healthy and happy marriage for the past thirty-five years."

Todd's story should be a wake-up call for us to follow Christ all the way, even when it feels uncomfortable. We cannot embrace cross-race friendships while rejecting interracial romance. If we do, there must be biblical grounds that support our behavior. Peter's and Brian's perspective of cross-race friendships were built on a weak foundation — one that lacked integrity, honesty, and openness of their true feelings toward Todd and biblical reconciliation.

I challenge you to courageously move beyond the aim of forming weak ties in your cross-race relationships. Different times call for different strategies! Our present-day reality is far removed from the black-white relational possibilities of the 1970s, when Granovetter's theory was developed. It's a new day now! Cross-race relationships that remain weak or surface level do not result in rewarding experiences. More important, aiming for weak ties does not line up with Jesus' command to "love one another. As I have loved you, so you must love one another" (John 13:34). I have seen too many healthy and strong cross-race friendships to settle for the goal of weak ties.

Admittedly, developing cohesive cross-race relationships will take time, perhaps even more time than it takes to form strong same-race friendships. It depends on your willingness to open your heart to someone else, as discussed in chapter 4. If you've taken the time to purchase this book, learn about racial attraction, and work through the forgiveness piece, you owe it to yourself to expect nothing less than to form strong ties with people of other races. It is not impossible, nor is it a one-in-a-million game of chance.

THE MARKS OF STRONG CROSS-RACE RELATIONSHIPS

Jesus is repulsed by lukewarmness. He wants us to either be hot (passionate in our service of His kingdom) or cold (definitive about our unwillingness to serve Him). He clearly tells us that if we are lukewarm, He will spew us out of His mouth (see Revelation 3:15-16). These are strong words. One thing is clear: Jesus wants true followers — men and women who fit the biblical standard of being a disciple, an ardent follower. In the same way, the lifestyle of a disciple as it pertains to cross-race relationships requires a strong commitment. We must aim for forming strong ties in our interethnic relationships in the same way we aim to form a strong tie with Jesus Christ in prayer, worship, and service.

When a cross-race relationship is strong and healthy, it is cohesive. To have a cohesive cross-race relationship, you need to:

1. Contemplate racial questions.
2. Protect your cross-race friends.
3. Model commitment to diversity.
4. Entertain racially diverse houseguests.
5. Commit to long-term friendship.
6. Keep the relationship healthy.
7. Practice self-sacrifice.

When you practice these seven behaviors and live out these values in your cross-race relationships, your friendships will grow, deepen, and naturally form into a strong and cohesive bond. Let's take a closer look at each of these.

1. Contemplate racial questions.

When questions about race and race-related issues are entertained in a nondefensive manner, the relationship offers a sense of safety. Racial inquiry is not considered offensive.

That was the case for Mercedes, a Puerto Rican woman, and her friend Ruth, a Korean. Mercedes told me, "I was able to tell her some of my prejudices and ask questions about Asian people. I openly confessed how I'd picked up and carried myths about Asian women because of the brainwashing of the media. For example, I thought that all Asian girls were thin and looked like Barbie dolls. It wasn't until I was able to openly share my suspicions and even faulty opinions that I adjusted my views. Ruth helped me realize that Asian women struggle with their weight like the rest of the population. I learned that they also have the same fears and insecurities as everybody else. Our relationship has brought my faith into reality in the area of race relations."

2. Protect your cross-race friends.

The relationship becomes strong as you function as an advocate for your cross-race friend. Advocates must freely communicate the position of their friends whether in their presence or not. This means that you refuse to sit idly by while anyone gossips or maligns the character of your cross-race friends on any grounds, particularly one of race. I'm not suggesting that you defend someone who is wrong. What I am saying is that when people are not present to defend themselves, no one has the right to tear them down. You won't be silent if someone makes an off-color or racial crack; instead, you will object because you want to defend your friend's race or ethnicity.

If you remain silent, it could be interpreted as being in agreement with the racial slur. Just as your attorney would not be your attorney for long if he allowed the opposing party's counsel or even the judge to say incorrect things about you, you will not maintain your cross-race relationships without advocacy.

Thomas Kochman, professor of communication and theater at the University of Illinois, said, "When I meet minority students in my classes for the first time, I know that where I stand with respect to issues and my personal philosophy will be as important to them as what I know about their language and culture. I also know that I need to indicate where I am going with the information. Consequently, information is presented not just as an interesting set of facts but for the sake of argument. Argument in turn is presented for the sake of persuasion, and persuasion for the sake of social change."[4]

This is why being an advocate means that you know the position of your cross-race friends on matters of diversity so you can present *their* argument as if they were present to defend themselves. This practice demonstrates your commitment to diversity.

3. Model commitment to diversity.

This behavior is not specific to a particular person like trait 2 is. It is behavior that guards the overall concept and belief that says, "I am totally committed to modeling diversity."

As you live out this value, your cross-race friends and professional colleagues will know where you stand both philosophically and behaviorally. You will have to determine how you're going to respond when racial slurs and off-color racial jokes are spewed in your presence. This trait conveys that you are uncomfortable with any level of hypocrisy. Either you are a friend of diversity or a foe of it. You cannot be a silent bystander of such social crimes and expect your cross-race relationships to be strong. You have to be the same person with your same-race friends that you are with your cross-race friends. Compartmentalizing your preference for diversity is not an option.

Sherri grew up in an all-white town, in an all-white school system. The first time she met people of other cultures and races was in college. Despite the fact that her father was a bigot who hammered into her that whites are superior to others, Sherri was drawn to people of other cultures. She wanted to learn about them, their interests, and their customs. This was put to the test when the college paired her with a Chinese roommate. In a small-group Bible study, Sherri shared, "My Chinese roommate helped me to understand that people—all kinds of people—have the same common needs: the need for belonging, love, and respect. My father's views remained *his* views and not mine." Sherri's choice to learn about and love her roommate modeled a commitment to diversity.

4. Entertain racially diverse houseguests.

When you open your home to a cross-race friend, it strengthens your relationship. When Arpita emigrated from India to the States to attend graduate school in Connecticut, she felt extremely disconnected and isolated. A foreign student with limited cross-racial experience, she did not know how to connect with the largely white population at her school. Her only plan was to continue her faith by finding a good Christian church.

As providence would have it, Susan — a classmate of Swedish descent — introduced Arpita to the church where she worshipped. Susan immediately empathized with Arpita. Her mother had emigrated from Sweden to the States and over the years had shared stories of the loneliness foreigners feel when they first arrive in a new country.

Susan was Arpita's first friend of a different race. The relationship developed into something special because Susan went out of her way to invite Arpita to her home to meet her mother. Arpita became like a sister to Susan. The guest room was Arpita's bedroom during holidays and school breaks. Susan quickly discovered that her friendship with Arpita was going to yield rich benefits. Arpita is a focused and mentally tough woman who does not give up in the face of hardships. From her, Susan learned how to be a fighter, something she'd struggled her entire life to become. In return, Susan taught Arpita about American culture.

5. Commit to long-term friendship.

Relationships grow strong when cross-race friends make a clear commitment to the durability of the relationship. Making a commitment is not a one-time action; it is saying yes to the many opportunities that promote the development of the friendship.

Some of these opportunities will be enjoyable, while others might be more challenging. For instance, you might be invited to attend a graduation party for your cross-race friend's daughter. By celebrating the accomplishments of your friend's daughter, you bring goodwill to the relationship. You will also add more goodwill when your friend's wife has a devastating illness and you absorb his unpredictable mood swings. Your commitment to the relationship during this strained season will likely strengthen it even more.

One of the benefits of having long-term cross-race friendships is that in time, you will no longer think of the relationship as a cross-race relationship. You simply see it as a relationship. Your unconscious perspective is a cross-cultural one. In other words, you don't have to concentrate on maintaining a cross-cultural outlook because it has become your natural response, in the same way that chewing is a natural response after taking a bite of food.

In his book *Blink*, Malcolm Gladwell says that psychologists have begun to look more closely at the role unconscious, or implicit, associations play in our beliefs and behavior. He talks about a fascinating tool called the Implicit Association Test (IAT). The IAT assesses the connections we make "between pairs of ideas that are already related in our mind."[5] It does not connect pairs of ideas that are unfamiliar to us even if we want them to be familiar. There is a Race IAT, which measures your unconscious attitude toward race, and it has been found that it might be different from your conscious attitude. It would be interesting to know if there is a direct correlation between a cohesive cross-race relationship and an individual's unconscious attitude about race. Do you think that your unconscious attitude and your conscious attitude toward race are the same? If you have a few minutes, give it a whirl by logging on to https://implicit.harvard.edu/implicit/research/ to see how you fare.

6. Keep the relationship healthy.

Emotionally healthy cross-race relationships do not allow personality or cultural clashes to go unaddressed. The two people are constantly talking about life and the value they place on relationships in an attempt to smooth out any hiccups. At times, there must be a loving confrontation in order to keep one another honest about their actions, values, and feelings.

Working in the information technology department of a large university afforded Korean-born Hyun Jae the opportunity to connect across racial and cultural lines. The first thing she did was tell everyone to call her Jane rather than try to have them pronounce Hyun Jae, which means *wise* and *respect* in Korean. Jane's Christian commitment was quite noticeable to her colleagues in the way she respectfully treated them even when tempers flared because of stress. Carolyn, an African-American woman, took a liking to Jane and was drawn to her inner beauty and confidence. During their frequent conversations at the lunch table, they began to discuss the topic of faith in Christ. In a few months, despite her newness to cross-racial relationships, Jane led Carolyn to Christ.

Carolyn's Muslim background periodically pulled her back to the mosque in an attempt to process a difficult aspect of her life. One day she confided in Jane by admitting her religious confusion and conflict in worldviews. She also confessed that she was periodically making poor moral choices, which she knew did not please God. Jane, a member of Christ Church, shared with me how close she felt to Carolyn because her confession demonstrated integrity, even though she was struggling to live out her new faith.

Fortunately, Jane was able to help Carolyn straighten out the sticking points in her faith. This helped her become a more devoted follower of Christ. In striving to maintain an honest and healthy relationship, Jane was also demonstrating the cross-cultural reach of the gospel. Imagine if every Christ follower walked out Jesus' call to live cross-culturally. Not only would we experience a better society but the gospel message would spread more rapidly across cultural and racial lines.

7. Practice self-sacrifice.

Cross-race relationships thrive when there is a willingness to support one another during times of crisis. This sacrificial behavior occurs when gifts are given, financial assistance is made, and convenience is suspended for the sake of another's well-being. One Filipino woman told me that if it were not for her white friend Mildred, she would not have been able to cope with the unexpected death of her husband. Gladys recalled, "The regular phone calls and frequent visits to the hospital Mildred made to help me cope with my husband's illness and subsequent death was my lifeline. I will never forget her unselfish display of love and friendship during that dark period of my life."

Although such traits as self-sacrifice can be recognized only over time, they must have a starting point. There is no greater place to start than where you are today, and there is never a convenient time to model self-sacrifice. That's probably why it's called self-sacrifice. Self-sacrifice means changing plans and inconveniencing yourself without drawing attention to your thoughtfulness. Once you begin forming a cross-race relationship, nurture it by learning to give of yourself so that your friendship can grow strong and cohesive.

GETTING STARTED

A Native-American grandfather was talking to his grandson. He said, "I feel as if I have two wolves fighting in my heart. One wolf is vengeful, angry, and violent. The other wolf is just the opposite: He's loving and compassionate." The grandson asked, "Which wolf will win the fight in your heart?" The grandfather answered, "The one I feed." Similarly, strong cross-race relationships occur because you feed them through the seven traits outlined in the previous section.

These seven indicators did not emerge from a theoretical laboratory; I uncovered them as I talked with people about their relationships. These true-to-life reconcilers started from the same point as you: ground zero. Sure, these people may seem much further along the cross-cultural journey, but the key is that they decided to start the journey. Their obedience to answer Jesus' call to love their neighbors as themselves has resulted in fantastic experiences.

Deciding to initiate cross-race relationships is the hardest part. It means that you must leave your comfort zone. This occurs when you create a sense of urgency by telling yourself, *It's time. No more excuses. I must pursue strong ties across racial lines.*

You can decide to change today! In fact, change may have been percolating deep within your soul for quite some time. The moso bamboo plant of China and the Far East is known for its remarkable growth; you may experience the same kind of sudden success. After the moso is planted, no visible growth occurs for up to five years, even under ideal conditions. Then, as if by magic, the moso plant suddenly begins growing at the rate of nearly two-and-a-half feet per day. It commonly reaches a full height of ninety feet within only six weeks. It's not magic. The moso's rapid growth is due to the miles of roots it develops during those first five years of life. No one was aware that the plant was getting ready for powerful growth during the past five years. Similarly, you may have been getting ready to build healthy cross-race relationships although you offered no visible signs. Your values and passion for diversity are akin to a root system that is unseen but very real. Now it's time to live out the principles.

MODELING RECONCILIATION

Many Christians are guilty of idolizing Bible characters. As we read the Bible, we unconsciously give some characters credit for things they never accomplished. Peter is credited, and rightly so, for accomplishing a lot of good for the kingdom of God. In the arena of faith, he was the only disciple to climb out of the safety of the boat and walk on water at Jesus' command. Although Peter did not complete the journey on the water, we have to give him his props: He did walk on water!

Peter also courageously stood up and preached Christ on the day of Pentecost in front of thousands of people. Many in the crowds were gripped with perplexity, others laughed in scorn, and some mocked out of confusion because of the believers speaking in tongues after receiving the baptism of the Holy Spirit. In response to Peter's spontaneous sermon, approximately three thousand people came to Christ that day (see Acts 2:41). Peter can be credited with a lot. But one thing God rebuked him for was his failure to model diversity.

Peter was visiting Antioch, Paul's home church, for a short

spell. The city of Antioch was a thriving metropolis and a safe haven for the cross-cultural church of the same name that Paul and Barnabas founded (see Acts 11:19-30). Both were seasoned cross-cultural leaders who knew the ins and outs of cross-race relationships. Peter was a mature spiritual leader but immature in navigating the murky waters of diversity. As Scripture puts it,

> When Peter came to Antioch, [Paul] opposed him to his face, because he was clearly in the wrong. Before certain men came from James, he used to eat with the Gentiles. But when they arrived, he began to draw back and separate himself from the Gentiles because he was afraid of those who belonged to the circumcision group. The other Jews joined him in his hypocrisy, so that by their hypocrisy even Barnabas was led astray. (Galatians 2:11-13)

The actions of a leader — or anyone, for that matter — is critical to the culture of an organization, just as the action of a parent sets the tone for the family. Paul had no recourse other than to challenge Peter in front of everyone. Peter's behavior was creating racial unrest within the congregation. He chose to eat with only Jewish believers, ignoring the fellowship of Gentile Christians. Because Peter's infraction was public and overt, Paul's correction had to be public and direct. The call to model reconciliation is not an individual choice. You cannot self-select to ignore God's mandate. No one can, not even the great apostle Peter. The impact is too serious.

YOU HAVE TO OVERCOME PERSONAL FEAR

Peter's reticence in mingling with the Gentiles (the umbrella term to mean all those who are non-Jewish) was very apparent.

When Peter was the only Jewish leader from the Jerusalem church at Antioch, he freely engaged with the Gentiles at Antioch. But the moment others came from Jerusalem, he began to consciously and noticeably pull back to the point of total separation. Paul knew the deal. Peter was uncomfortable and wanted to save face with his Jewish buddies by maintaining the kind of monocultural lifestyle he'd become accustomed to in Jerusalem. Behind Peter's discomfort was fear. He was afraid of what the other Jews would think. He was afraid of what they would tell the guys back home. Peter's fear got the best of him.

I wonder if his fear was also an indicator that he'd not yet worked out a defendable theology regarding cross-race friendships. I wonder if he was uncomfortable because he did not see sufficient value in connecting cross-racially. Was his discomfort simply an attempt to save face, or were other issues lurking in the dark parts of his heart that required a healthy challenge from a skilled cross-cultural leader?

What about you? What fears are keeping you from forming cross-race friendships? Consider your life and any internal struggles you might be facing regarding diversity. If no one challenges you, will you remain in a neutral or negative position for the rest of your life? This book may be your sole challenge, so don't dismiss the tough things I must now say.

YOU KNOW TOO MUCH TO GO BACK

If you choose to refrain from living out what you now know about cross-race relationships, you will find yourself struggling with what psychologists call *cognitive dissonance*. This term describes the internal battle people face simply on the grounds that they believe one thing but live by a different set of values. Cognitive dissonance is illustrated when a married woman regularly rendezvoused with her secret lover while pretending to be happily married. Her husband may be unsuspecting of her hypocritical behavior, but she won't be able to live with her contradiction for long. Her mind will not bear up under the stress of cognitive dissonance, and sooner or later she will slip and call her husband by her lover's name or commit some other faux pas. God has so wired us that our minds will try to synchronize our two lives. This will also occur if you don't courageously choose to practice what you've learned.

If your beliefs hold to the fact that cross-race relationships are morally right, are ethically decent, and can be lived out practically, don't continue to limit your socializing within the safety of your own culture. You know too much now to consider that an option. This was the essence of Paul's argument to Peter. He said, "You are a Jew, yet you live like a Gentile and not like a Jew. How is it, then, that you force Gentiles to follow Jewish customs?" (Galatians 2:14). He was telling Peter that his current lifestyle was more reflective of a Gentile's lifestyle in that he was not saddled with all of the Jews' rituals and customs he used to follow. Paul was challenging Peter to live as a complete Jew — one who had accepted Christ as his Messiah and discovered the fullness of this salvation and was compelled to lovingly share his life and faith beyond his culture.

This is our calling. This is our mandate. We are called to live with and love our neighbors — all of them. The antidote to the sickness of fear is love. The apostle John wrote, "There is no fear in love. But perfect love drives out fear, because fear has to do with punishment. The one who fears is not made perfect in love" (1 John 4:18). Paul was challenging Peter to see how his actions, which were driven by fear, needed the therapeutic and corrective power of love.

TAKE YOUR PLACE AS A LEADER IN RECONCILIATION

It has been said that leadership is influence. True. Equally true is this statement: "Everyone influences at least one other person." Right now there are people watching you to learn what *they* must do regarding cross-race relationships. Whether you like it or not, it is a reality and there's nothing you can do about it.

So why not rise to the occasion and give them something worthwhile to follow? It's easy to ascribe the responsibility of reconciliation to world leaders, organizational presidents, and celebrities, but the stark reality is that reconciliation is everybody's responsibility! This is the rationale and perspective of authentic reconcilers. Once you've become comfortable with the notion that you should build and maintain cross-race relationships, the next vital step is to help others share that same value. True reconcilers want to be part of the solution to social reform. The reconciler's challenge, which is also a leadership challenge, is to personally influence others to live cross-culturally.

Paul's anger toward Peter hinged on the fact that Peter's improper behavior was influencing others within their community, including Barnabas, who was a strong cross-cultural leader. When Barnabas and the other Jews joined Peter in his hypocrisy, it communicated that they too were unclear as to what it meant to please God. Perhaps if Peter did not have the stature he held, Barnabas and the others would not have fallen prey to his misguided behavior. But Peter did have clout. His actions were interpreted as if he was being Spirit-directed, when all along he was wrong about how to live as an authentic reconciler.

Paul recognized how dangerous Peter's actions were. That's why he could not excuse his behavior or correct him in private. Racism encourages deep-seated emotions. It awakens feelings, passions, and sentiments that may have been stuffed down deep into the recesses of our hearts. Although we may ignore these feelings during good times, during times of uncertainty (such as the O. J. Simpson trial and the 2009 Professor Gates and Sergeant Crowley debacle that created racial unrest across our nation), the unresolved racial issues come bursting out of hiding. With the kind of unrest one racial act can trigger, Paul had to act fast. An unchecked prejudiced behavior from a visible leader could have upset the entire cross-race culture the Antioch church enjoyed.

Peter had to be challenged. The people had to know that Peter was not acting in line with the teachings of Jesus or modeling the values of a reconciler. His influence in this matter had to be short-circuited.

If you can influence others, you can also lead them. Leadership is influence. It is the ability to use your personality, skill, and know-how to influence and enlist the support of others in the advancement of a vision they have come to personally embrace as a worthy cause. They might not share your passion or your vision the first time they hear it, but due to your influence, their hearts change and they soon adopt your goal as their own. This ability to influence others with what you're passionate about indicates that you've answered the call to leadership.

Living a quiet and exemplary life connected with other ethnic groups is good and noble, but it is not the pinnacle of being a reconciler. Fully engaged reconcilers are gripped with the reality that they must be in the business of changing the world, one person at a time. Their marching orders are to reform society by reforming people's views concerning diversity. Just as distinct levels of racial prejudice and ethnic injustice exist in the world, varying levels of racial reconciliation and positive cross-race proponents must also exist. You must take your place at the seat of leadership and help communicate the challenge for all to be reconcilers, especially those who claim to be Christ followers.

In his book *The Nature of Prejudice*, renowned Harvard sociologist Gordon Allport defines prejudice as *prejudgment with emotions*. In essence, he says that someone who is guilty of prejudging another also has strong negative emotions tied into his or her prejudgment. Therefore, eliminating the outward actions that broadcast a prejudiced person's prejudgment may not necessarily eliminate that individual's strong negative emotions. Prejudice is a deep-rooted and deep-seated issue that requires work to successfully conquer.

Allport goes on to identify five levels of prejudice: (1) talking about it with friends, (2) avoiding a certain group, (3) excluding all members of the group from social privileges, employment opportunity, residential housing, and so on, (4) physically attacking members of the group, and (5) exterminating the group (massacres, lynching, ethnic cleansings).[1] As you can see, prejudice is not only damaging to the one who is caught in its ugly clutches; it grows to devastating levels of societal impact. Left unchecked in the human heart, even at the seemingly private and mild stage of level one, prejudice has the potential to grow into the violent and catastrophic stage of level five.

The Bible offers a wonderful outlook about combating evil in the human heart: "Where sin increased, grace [God's empowering presence] increased all the more" (Romans 5:20). This verse helps us see that building cross-race connections can increase more quickly than any form of prejudice. But, for this to happen, you must step up your expectation and personal commitment to influence the cross-cultural practices of others.

Imagine what our world would look like if you and others like you expected people to advance up the ladder of what I call the five levels of reconciliation. We would graduate (1) from merely talking about making cross-race connections with our same-race friends (2) to including all groups in our circle of friends (3) to including all members of other groups in social privileges, employment opportunity, and residential housing (4) to demonstrating tangible acts of love to members of other groups, and finally (5) to practicing social justice, ensuring equity and equal rights, and protecting ethnic survivability in order to build up groups who've experienced large-scale ethnic abuses.

YOUR INFLUENCE STARTS IN SEED FORM

For these distinct degrees of cross-race practices to appear in your life, you must embrace a deep conviction toward multiculturalism. The three stages of growth associated with plant life can be readily used as a pattern for maturing your cross-race influence from level one to level five. First, there is the seed that must be planted for germination to occur. Second, the plant grows and matures. Third, the plant bears fruit. Not everyone will become a level-five reconciler and reverse such egregious damages as ethnic cleansing, but everyone can certainly fulfill their growth potential and bear fruit. At the outset, you won't know how much fruit you can eventually produce, but the aim is to maximize your growth potential.

Bill Hybels, pastor of the 24,000-member Willow Creek Community Church (South Barrington, Illinois), often refers to God's challenge for him to embrace reconciliation as his *second conversion.*[2] The shock of knowing that his previous view of the world was a monocultural one could be framed only as "I was converted for a second time." This realization and the willingness to change suggested that the seed of reconciliation had germinated within his soul. This second conversion is akin to the germination of a seed.

Germination moves a person from having a predominance of same-race friends to welcoming cross-race relationships into his or her social circle. At this beginning stage, the fruit of reconciliation is still in seed form. Just as moisture activates the germination process for the seed, discovering the benefits of cross-race friendships awakens the soul to diversity.

The early stage of your growth as a reconciler is primarily internal. You're the only one being influenced by what you are reading, hearing, sensing, and perceiving as your new reality. Your values are being transformed from a monoracial or possibly ethnocentric one to a global and multicultural one. In this first stage of influence, your new values are formed. Values are an integral part of your daily life. They dictate, determine, standardize, and change your relations with family, friends, organizations, community, and society. Values are a powerful source of life and behavior. In fact, your values will cause your influence to grow from its fledging state to the next level of authority.

As your newfound values mature, you will develop a passion for a new way of thinking, behaving, and living. Life feels exciting again! New experiences await you. Suddenly you are moved to share your new knowledge with others. You realize that you can influence others to rethink their positions on diversity simply by posing the very questions you had to grapple with, such as, "How can you ignore people simply on the grounds that they look different from you? Why is it acceptable for you to think of yourself as superior to the next guy just because you are from a different culture?" Such questions have the ability to change one's life, and a good question can challenge someone to rethink an essential part of his or her life.

This truth is illustrated in a story theologian William Barclay told about a group of World War II soldiers. The soldiers had lost a friend in battle and wanted to give their fallen comrade a decent burial. They found a church with a graveyard behind it, surrounded by a white fence. They asked the parish priest if their friend could be buried in the church's graveyard.

"Was he Catholic?" the priest inquired.

"No, he was not," answered the soldiers.

"I'm sorry, then," said the priest. "Our graveyard is reserved for members of the holy church. But you can bury your friend outside the fence. I will see that the gravesite is cared for."

"Thank you, Father," said the soldiers, and they proceeded to bury their friend just outside the graveyard, on the other side of the fence.

When the war ended, the soldiers decided to visit the

gravesite of their friend before returning home. They remembered the location of the church and the grave, just outside the fence. They searched for it but couldn't find it. Finally, they went to the priest to inquire about its location.

"Sir, we cannot find our friend's grave."

"Well," answered the priest, "after you buried your fallen friend, it just didn't seem right to me that he should be buried outside the fence."

"So you moved his grave?" asked the soldiers.

"No," said the priest. "I moved the fence."[3]

The question *What qualifies a man to be buried within the cemetery?* stimulated the priest's thinking, indicating that his conscience was troubled. Questions are a great way to get people thinking and are a wonderful, nonthreatening tool that influences people.

NO MORE EXCUSES

Remember, just as there are five levels that reflect the depth of prejudice in the human heart, there are five stages that reflect your intensity of appreciation for diversity. Even if you are at the beginning stage of your new worldview, you can effectively influence others, as the following story illustrates.

At a festive backyard barbecue, two men shared with me their personal stories of mistakes and triumphs; one man was white and the other African-American. The men had become good friends over the years because they shared a common past. They were cellmates in prison. Both had made wrong choices that were drug related. Both had accepted Christ as their Savior prior to their imprisonment, but their wrong choices with marijuana and crack cocaine led to an expensive drug habit neither could afford except through robbery and other criminal activities. As they shared their stories with me, they focused on their healing and the joy of freedom — freedom in Christ and now freedom from prison.

When Ken, the African-American man, was placed in the cell, Frank, the white brother, had been there for a year. Frank had his shirt off, and the swastika tattooed on his chest was clearly visible. The moment Ken saw it, he demanded that the guard place him in another cell. "We'll kill each other," he said. "Give me another cell. This guy hates black people!" The guard ignored his complaints and walked away, leaving the two inmates to settle their grievances in the way prisoners so often do. Frank quickly realized what had caused Ken's irritation and said, "Hey, man, don't worry. I'm no longer the guy this swastika says I am. I'm a born-again Christian and love people of all races."

Ken was shocked. He quickly told Frank, "I'm born-again also." As we ate our hamburgers that afternoon, both Frank and Ken told me how they sang worship songs together in their cell to celebrate their joy in Christ. Ken regularly played his guitar, and the two men lifted their voices in harmony to the Lord. I walked away from that cookout amazed once again at God. His powerful grace enters into the darkest part of our lives to rescue us from the sin of prejudice and convert us into reconcilers.

If God can use Frank and Ken to model reconciliation in prison, what excuse do we have for disobeying the call of Christ to build bridges to other cultures? We have none. Just as Frank was unable to change the tattoo of his past, we may not be able to change aspects of our pasts. But he was able to surrender to Jesus his heart of prejudice and racial isolation so the passions of a reconciler could be birthed in him. We can do the same. The ability to live cross-culturally comes about only because we have surrendered ourselves to Jesus' challenge to model reconciliation.

I have grown significantly because someone loved me enough to get in my face and challenge me to step up my leadership. I'm convinced that many of us don't fulfill our potential because no one challenges us. Nobel Peace Prize winner Viktor Frankl said, "What man actually needs is not a tensionless state but rather the striving and struggling for some goal worthy of him. What he needs is not the discharge of tension at any cost but the call of a potential meaning waiting to be fulfilled by him."[4] The tension you may be feeling right now to live cross-culturally will help you live up to your potential. Use the tension as a propeller that will lift you up in cross-cultural success.

The Bible uses two metaphors to describe Christians who practice their spiritual experience on a societal level: salt and light (see Matthew 5:13-16). *Salt* speaks of a preservative, and *light* represents goodness and righteousness. Jesus used these terms to describe the type of lasting positive change possible in society when individuals set out to impact the lives of people within their sphere of influence. If we are to see cross-cultural friendliness blossom in our generation, every Christian must take Jesus' marching orders to heart. Reconciliation is not a choice—it's a mandate!

The time for excuses in the area of race relations and cross-cultural friendship is behind us. Too much is at stake. The next generation needs a better world, a more loving world, a more just world. They need you and me to step up our game and dismiss the excuses that we've become comfortable in making. We've memorized our rationalizations to the point that they sound like a rap song's hook. I invite you to instead rehearse what you know to be the heart of God. Providing influence in the area of race relations is everyone's responsibility.

The challenge to lead always comes at the most awkward times. Gandhi had no choice but to lead despite the size of the British power structure. Dr. Martin Luther King Jr. had no recourse but to lead even when the threat of death constantly loomed over him. The cry of social injustice could not be avoided no matter how much he hoped, prayed, and tried to keep his own personal life focused upon good Christian values. He had to lead!

It's easy to cry silently or even at the top of your lungs, "We need to start loving each other!" But too many people have done that—are doing that—and still we've made little change.

It's time for you to leave the classroom and walk out into the cool, crisp daylight of life and live what you believe is true and godly. Yield to that holy frustration, that righteous anger, that makes you want to bellow at the top of your lungs, "No more excuses! Today I will start living a cross-cultural life!"

CHAPTER 9

A PLACE TO STAND

Many years ago, I had a speaking engagement in Flensburg, Germany, in the northern part of the country, where farmland and windmills adorn the countryside. After one of the evening meetings, my team and I were quite hungry. My host, who was fluent in German and English, joyously hopped into his car to drive to the nearest restaurant, an hour away. A friendly German who didn't speak a single word of English got into a second car. He simply smiled, big and often.

My entire team piled into the car driven by my bilingual host. The other car was empty except for the wide-smiling driver, eager to have someone accompany him. I jumped into his car, and off we went. The road was pitch-black, especially out in the country where streetlights were nowhere to be found. As we inched our way through the darkness to get to the highway, I noticed the pungent aroma of flowers mixed with the downwind smell of animals. My senses of sight and smell were heightened because there was total silence inside the car. My host did not speak English and I did not speak German, so we drove in complete silence. We both wished we could talk, laugh, and get to know one another, but the only

German words I was able to remember were *Ich spreche kein Deutsch*, which means, "I don't speak German." My driver knew a couple of English words, which he periodically said to me in his strong German accent: "I don't speak English." As we drove for the next hour, once in a while we turned to each other and laughed as he said, "I don't speak English," and I responded, "*Ich spreche kein Deutsch.*"

At the time, I didn't feel that we had connected, as we couldn't talk with each other. Looking back now, I would say we really did connect. Our hearts connected because we both *wanted* to talk to each other, laugh together about something funny, pass the time by learning tidbits about one another's family.

It's easy to understand why my American friends piled into the car of the bilingual driver. Why put yourself through the experience of having to quietly sit with someone who doesn't understand you and whom you don't understand? But in the world of diversity, someone has to make the first move, and I want to be that someone.

STANDING ON THE FOUNDATION OF LOVE

Reconciliation requires that you have a place to stand—a strong, secure place from which you can demonstrate to someone different from you, *I love you.* This is the cornerstone to launching into a cross-cultural friendship. The other person must feel the heat of your desire to walk across the ethnic divide and find strong footing on which to stand. These cross-cultural opportunities are everywhere; you just need to be observant and willing to walk through the doorway into someone else's world.

That is part of the message in the biblical story of the Good Samaritan (see Luke 10:25-37), one of the best known of all the parables. It depicts a kindhearted Samaritan caring for a complete stranger who had been beaten by thieves and left to die. The term *Good Samaritan* was originally coined from this biblical story and has long been used to label behavior that is virtuous toward a stranger in need. Jesus told the parable in response to a lawyer's intricate question, "Who is my neighbor?" While the question was designed to trap Jesus, the story demonstrates the fundamental principles of faith, compassion, equality, and love Jesus prescribed for humankind. These qualities, which the Bible recommends that society practice, originate from the commandments "Love the Lord your God with all your heart and with all your soul and with all your strength and with all your mind" and "Love your neighbor as yourself" (see verse 27).

The place of love is unshakeable. It gives you a firm footing, no matter your race, gender, economic situation, or level of cross-cultural experience. Love constructs strong cross-cultural friendships. Love, according to Jesus' parable, is not the mushy, gooey type that has no substance and body to it. Love is practical, helpful, and action oriented. It demonstrates outwardly the inner concerns of the heart. That is the kind of love the Good Samaritan demonstrated toward the wounded man. If most people in society lived by this principle, we would achieve what I call "the good society."

Jesus emphasized the preferred behavior of the Good Samaritan over that of two religious leaders: a Levite and a priest. These two clerics did absolutely nothing to aid the wounded man. They walked on the other side of the road, free from concern, guilt, and moral responsibility. This unconscionable behavior highlights the action of isolationism, which calls for every person to be out for himself. Jesus strongly denounced this attitude as destructive to the formation of a good society and as counterproductive to building cross-cultural relationships. The key to building a good society is the revitalization of marketplace ethics, education, social movements, family, and faith.

If we are to see the good society achieved in America, the institutions of the family, business and economics, and religion (more specifically, the Christian church) must be reshaped. We cannot continue to wait for the next guy to make the first move. We have to see ourselves as the next guy. We have to make the first move. Each person must practice the virtues exemplified by the Good Samaritan, regardless of the race, ethnicity, culture, or religion of the persons in need.

LOVE YOUR NEIGHBOR

In a good society, the solution is to love your neighbor and not merely tolerate him or her. In the parable of the Good Samaritan, the lawyer seemed to be asking Jesus, "Does the command to love your neighbor as yourself extend to other races, or even to those who are not considered to be God's covenant people?" Jesus' answer could perhaps be summarized like this: "Love other people — rich people, poor people, victimized people, and even Samaritans — as yourself. Love them as if they were just like you. Do not segregate your love." The parable of the Good Samaritan omitted the wounded man's race, ethnicity, and religious affiliation. Jesus' purpose was to get His audience to think through the primary issues of love, compassion, and humanitarian concern rather than focus on the nonessentials.

The parable should be a snapshot of what reconciliation and cross-cultural relationships look like in your own life, including the professional and social areas. First-century lawyers, similar to their modern counterparts and today's businesspeople, were experts at finding loopholes that allowed them to escape God's straightforward commands for forming a good society. In this particular parable, the lawyer did not ask Jesus to define *neighbor* simply because he was curious. The lawyer had already worked out his answer, which undoubtedly was prepared in order to excuse him from the simple mandate to love his neighbor.

The commands of God are simple. Jesus said, "Love God and love your neighbor." How does Christ's command to love your neighbor as yourself apply to segregation, racially divided churches, integrated schools, and minorities in the inner city? If your answer contains a dozen qualifying footnotes, obscuring the simple command of God to love your neighbor, it's likely that you feel about other races the same way the Jewish lawyer felt about the Samaritans: tolerant. And, according to my earlier definition of *tolerance*, this really means intolerance. Jesus was addressing this parable to people whose intolerance caused them to ignore the cry of victimized people living in their midst. Therefore, the way to heal the faltering efforts of forming cross-cultural relationships in the workplace or in the broader, communal part of your life is to love your neighbor as you love yourself.

The practical outworking of this love is in making pay scales of minorities equal to pay scales of their white male counterparts. It is also manifested through laws and mandatory sensitivity-training workshops for employees as a means of safeguarding the equal treatment of people within America's multiethnic workplace. Loving your neighbor as yourself is seen when you sit next to someone of a different race in the cafeteria or invite that person to lunch. Love is demonstrated when you go out of your way to connect with someone you normally would shy away from because of the outward difference of race. As the parable of the Good Samaritan demonstrates, physical and financial assistance to the needy stranger is part of the neighborly responsibility of the global community in a good society. If you are unable to help someone else because of your own tight financial circumstance, you can still display your love by spending time with that person over a cup of coffee. Ask God to show you a practical way to reach across the cultural aisle to love your neighbor. The Lord always answers those kinds of prayers.

TEACH YOUR FAMILY WHERE TO STAND

The family is the cradle of cultural scripting because parents model the acceptable cultural behavior, norms, and communication rules they desire to pass on to their children.[1] Our perspectives on life and our viewpoints about certain aspects of social behavior are part of our cultural legacies. Since the 1960s, American society has seen a breakdown in the traditional family structure. Divorce numbers have doubled since 1960 and, according to the social science data, "since 1970 the marriage rate has fallen 30 percent while the divorce rate has climbed to 50 percent. Each year more than one million children live through the breakup of their families."[2] The demise of the family affects our ability to build cross-race friendships because the family is the first place of instruction on human values.

Because the family forms the underpinning of society, it bears the task of influencing and directing people. If families are to produce cross-cultural advocates who can bring reform to the multicultural marketplace, family members must practice the honesty, uprightness, and ethics required to engender trust within the hearts of their multiethnic colleagues.

If American families will incorporate the behavioral practices of kindness, neighborly concern, mercy, compassion, and love demonstrated by the Good Samaritan, we will be closer to achieving the good society. The wounded man had been robbed and beaten half to death. His wounds were not self-inflicted. This is a simple observation but an important one.

Many factors have brought wounded people to where they are. People do not choose to become victims. They are usually caught up in a current too powerful to overcome. The assumption that individuals or groups are responsible for their own victimization is usually an excuse used to sidestep the mandate to love your neighbor as yourself. Sadly, those who hold this perspective simply pass by the wounded on the other side of the road, undisturbed by what they see.

Perhaps the priest and the Levite excused themselves because they did not view this man as a member of their own family but rather as a stranger who was somehow responsible for his situation. That is a convenient perspective to take when it comes to other people and their problems. But the mandate of the kingdom of God, which is shared by authentic reconcilers, is to show mercy without assessing blame. The story of the Good Samaritan illustrates what should happen when aspiring or well-established reconcilers are confronted with the suffering and needs of others. They should treat them as family members, regardless of their race, ethnicity, and culture.

The extension of mercy to members of our societal family will help tear down the walls of cultural isolation.

TEACH YOUR CHURCH FAMILY WHERE TO STAND

To achieve a good multicultural society, the church must embody the biblical teaching of being our brother's keeper (see Genesis 4:9). When we provide care and compassion to the global community, we carry out this mandate. The apostle Paul instructed us that "as we have opportunity, let us do good to *all* people, especially to those who belong to the family of believers" (Galatians 6:10, emphasis added). Scripture directs us to perform practical acts of love to all kinds of people, starting first within our own Christian community and then toward all of humanity.

Although I might not understand the sentiments of the Italian, Brazilian, Muslim, Hispanic, or German communities, if they are incensed about something, I have a moral obligation to become part of the solution to their problems. Because of my love for them, I must accommodate their feelings into my prayers and become sensitive to their plight. I am required by the dictates of the Bible to listen, to dialogue, and to see life from their perspective. Because we live together in one human family, I must ask my brothers and sisters of diverse worldviews and backgrounds, "What are some of the things you're going through? Are there things I do unconsciously that offend you? What can I do to help you feel united with me?" Cross-cultural communication requires that love be placed at the heart of understanding a person's values, beliefs, and customs.

As I mentioned earlier, Jesus never discussed the ethnic

origin or the religious affiliation of the wounded man in the parable of the Good Samaritan. That's because a robbery victim is a victim, regardless of nationality or religion. The reason the Samaritan stopped to offer help was that he felt compassion and empathy for the man. The Samaritan knew what it was like to be hated and rejected because of the history of racial prejudice levied against his ethnic group (see John 8:48). If the priest and Levite had allowed themselves to identify with the man in the ditch or consider how he must have felt, they would not have been so detached from his plight. When you identify with the problems and sufferings of others, it connects you with them. This is precisely what Jesus was getting at in the parable of the Good Samaritan.

Religious people are often intent on being right and pointing out the inaccurate beliefs of everyone else. Yet, if we were equally committed to fulfilling the mandate to love our neighbors, the good society would not remain a fictitious place; it would be manifested in our midst. The church has a biblical mandate to establish reconciliation workshops, conferences, and sensitivity training for its members to promote unity in God's house. And, in a divided society, the church must model unity.

I FOUND A PLACE TO STAND

Throughout this book, I purposely have not disclosed my race or ethnicity. I did not want to bias you. As human beings, we have been wired to form opinions and conclusions of others based on their race. I didn't want you to categorize me, so I shared my heart without disclosing my race.

When I was ten years old, my house was firebombed. My

parents had recently purchased a small home in Rosedale, Queens, a bedroom community in the heart of New York City, after moving our family from Jamaica to the United States. Two weeks after our family moved in, five white teenage boys threw a Molotov cocktail into one of the bedroom windows of our new home — into my bedroom window. The gasoline bomb exploded, and I saw a wall of flames as the fire began to burn our house. I shouted to alert my family about the blaze. We all ran out of the house, frightened like never before.

I can still see the fire trucks pulling up and the firefighters scrambling to get the hose so that the fire could be extinguished. It seemed like a lifetime before they turned on the water and brought the fire under control. Finally, the blaze was out. As it turned out, only minor damage was done to our house. But that night a fire of uncertainty, confusion, bewilderment, and anger toward white people was kindled in my heart.

The hatred toward my family did not stop there. We had to have around-the-clock police surveillance because of the death threats we received from white families within the community. The firebombing made the evening news and became the talk of the region. And even though the five white boys were caught just a few days later, they were released without charge of any wrongdoing. The judge said that it was just a childish prank. Imagine that. This criminal act of vandalism, attempted murder, arson, a hate crime, and the list goes on, was ignored by our criminal system.

This was the first time I ever experienced prejudice, and I was troubled and confused by what had happened. What had my family done wrong? Why were we hated? What had we done to deserve such treatment from total strangers? Although my parents were hurt and disillusioned, they sat us children down and instructed us this way: "Don't hate white people because of what these boys did." But their words didn't register with me.

To me, anger seemed the only appropriate response to the injustice done to my family. My so-called neighbors had bombed our house. My so-called neighbors had tried to kill me. They had taught me to hate myself because I was black. They taught me that I was not loved, was not worth loving, and not even good enough to be tolerated. Racial prejudice was totally new to me. My small island nation did not prepare me for such things. I did not know how to view myself as a black kid in a predominantly white culture, much less as a despised child. The family next door to us wouldn't even speak to us. They moved away within a month of our living there because they did not want to live next door to a black family. So I grew up with a hole in my heart toward the need to build cross-cultural relationships or even recognize the need to love my neighbor as myself.

When I was twenty years old, something happened that changed all that. At 10:00 p.m. on July 6, 1982, I accepted Jesus Christ as my Lord and Savior. I prayed a simple prayer, which I later learned was the prayer of salvation. Alone in my dorm room, I simply said, *Lord, if You are real, come into my heart and change me.* I had heard the gospel message from some Christian friends who shared Jesus with me for an entire year before this experience. My conversion came on the heels of a one-year journey to understanding the meaning of life. I had concluded that there must be more to life than making money, marrying a pretty girl, and having a great career.

Though I had none of these things at that time, I saw them as empty goals. Despite all my attempts to straighten out these foolish Christians, I found myself joining them.

What was really amazing, though, was that the prayer of salvation didn't merely heal my sin-sick soul; it also healed me of the pain of victimization. I emerged from my dorm room as a new believer in Jesus and as a man healed of prejudice and confusion over how I would live and connect with others in our pluralistic and multicultural society. If God could heal me, He can heal anyone of any aspect of social pain. I soon discovered that the medicine Christ used to heal and inoculate me from the disease of prejudice was His love. Jesus set me free to love. He empowered me to love Him, myself, and my neighbors. I also learned that reconciliation occurs on these same three levels: upward, inward, and outward.

When we love upward, we demonstrate a clear and genuine love toward God, our Creator and Savior. It is He who created us and forgave us of our countless sins. Without God's initiating love for us while we were still sinners, we would not be able to embrace the cross, the symbol of His love. Jesus went to the cross as a gift of love. This is the upward, or vertical, dimension of love, from which stems all other forms of love.

When we love inwardly, we demonstrate an ability to love ourselves. If I hate myself, I am also saying that I've not been fearfully and wonderfully made by God (see Psalm 139:14). To live devoid of acknowledging ourselves favorably as God's handiwork is one of the greatest sins you can commit. It is as if you're calling God a liar and rejecting the truthfulness of His Word. On July 6, 1982, I learned to love myself. This inward love is not idolatry or ethnic worship; it stems from God.

The requirement to love outwardly—the neighborly kind of love—becomes easy once the other two dimensions of love are in good working order. Sometimes it requires a little coaching or persuading, but once we see the need for loving our neighbors, there is no turning back to a monocultural lifestyle that rejects reconciliation. Our salvation experience awakens an internal longing to practice reconciliation with all in our sphere of influence.

Let's show the world that the Christian community has the answer to racial and cultural divisions: a transformed life through Jesus Christ. Let's stand on the foundation of God's love.

CONCLUSION

A few years ago, I was speaking in Kenya. Like many of the African countries, this East African nation is very poor. The average monthly salary is equivalent to thirty American dollars. Imagine living on thirty bucks a month. I wouldn't know how to begin, what to do, or how I'd live. All the amenities we now consider staples—cell phones, cable TV, the Internet—would have to be eliminated. Compared to the average Kenyan, I am rich.

There must have been about ten thousand people attending the nightly meetings. People were hungry for the Word of God and a display of His power. The following day, I decided to take a stroll through the market across the street from the hotel. This was not one of those large American malls with huge stores and an elaborate parking garage. It was a dusty street filled with all kinds of foot traffic, people on bicycles, others pulling or peddling rickshaws filled with passengers on their way to work or home. The street buzzed with the excitement of bartering, which is normal for Kenyan street merchants trying to eke out a few Kenyan shillings from bargain-hunting shoppers.

This was my fifth trip to Kenya, so I was accustomed to the people, the poverty, and the excitement of haggling for a deal. And because I grew up in New York City, haggling was almost a sport. Sometimes I'd haggle just for fun. On previous trips, I left loaded down with wooden carvings and other souvenirs that family and friends had asked for. This particular day, I strolled up and down the street, gazing at the vendors' wares in search of something that piqued my interest. I was shopping for myself. I wanted something that would make a great conversation piece back home in the States.

I moved quickly from one stall to another, but nothing caught my eye. Finally, at the end of the long line of stalls, an old woman stepped in front of her makeshift countertop, laden with beads, small wooden carvings, stone-type necklaces, and other knickknacks. This petite woman wearing a tattered and stained dress greeted me with a friendly smile that showed she had a loving heart despite all the missing and corroded teeth. I figured that poverty had affected her dental health and possibly her overall health.

I was surprised when she greeted me by name. "How are you, Pastor Ireland?" And before I could answer, she asked, "How are your wife and your two daughters?" When I asked how she knew who I was, I discovered that she had been coming to the meetings where I was speaking. She had also been present at the meetings over the previous years when I spoke. And although Marlinda and my daughters hadn't yet accompanied me to Kenya, this woman remembered the personal stories I'd shared about them in my sermons.

Without hesitating, she grabbed a brown paper bag and placed three of her most precious necklaces into it. She smiled, again showing her missing teeth, gently handed me the bag, and said, "Please give this gift to your wife and daughters." I quickly rummaged through my pocket to find a crisp hundred-dollar bill to give her. A hundred American dollars equaled 9,280 Kenyan shillings, the equivalent to almost four months of income in Kenya. I found it, rolled it up quickly, and reached out to give it to her. "No thank you," she said, still smiling. Without even knowing the amount of my gift, she had refused the money. I was shocked.

"I just want to give you a gift for your family," she said. Then she said something I'll never forget: "Don't you think that poor people like giving to others? It makes me feel good to bless you." I quickly turned my gaze away from her eyes so she wouldn't see my tears, but my tears were flowing like a fountain. My soul was immediately awakened to the value of human dignity.

Because of my thoughts of her appearance and economic lack, I had unconsciously stripped this woman of her human dignity. I had attempted to deny her the glory and joy of freely giving to another. But instead, *she* taught me about human dignity. She taught me that her economic state didn't determine her dignity, worth, importance, and value to God or her value to me. She taught me to stop judging people by their externals and to judge them by their internals: the heart. She taught me that true generosity is based not only on one's ability to give but also, as Jesus Himself explained, on the ability to receive. In that moment, I learned that my act of generosity really reflected a *lack* of generosity.

When the Pharisees placed tithing above justice, mercy, and faithfulness (see Matthew 23:23-24), Jesus corrected them, telling them to reverse the order—to place justice, mercy, and faithfulness *above* tithing but not to neglect any of them because all four practices were essential in living for God. That day, I learned to place human dignity *above* generosity because of its order of importance. When we don't value the culture and ethnicity of others enough to form healthy cross-race relationships with them, we are placing other things above that of human dignity.

The Skin You Live In has given you tools to effectively engage and build healthy cross-cultural relationships in every arena of life. Now the choice is up to you. Will you refuse opportunities that fall into your lap, the way I almost did by refusing this woman's gift? Or will you allow others to exhibit their God-given human dignity by showing them respect, love, and value by forming friendships with them? It's up to you.

Start today! Admit to yourself, God, family, friends, and even the world that you are a reconciler. Let everyone know that your mission is to reconcile people to God, and people to people. You are a reconciler. Reconcile!

NOTES

INTRODUCTION

1. Sam Roberts, "Non-Hispanic Whites Are Now a Minority in the 23-County New York Region," *The New York Times,* March 27, 2011, http://www.nytimes.com/2011/03/28/nyregion/28nycensus.html.
2. William B. Gudykunst and Young Yun Kim, *Communicating with Strangers: An Approach to Intercultural Communication* (New York: McGraw-Hill, 1997), 17.
3. George Barna, *Today's Pastor: A Revealing Look at What Pastors Are Saying About Themselves, Their Peers and the Pressures They Face* (Ventura, CA: Regal, 1993), 44.
4. C. Peter Wagner, *Church Growth: The State of the Art* (Wheaton, IL: Tyndale, 1986), 53.
5. David D. Ireland, "Minority Perspectives of Interracial Relationships in Large Multiracial Churches" (PhD diss., Regent University, 2002).

CHAPTER 1: LEAVING YOUR COMFORT ZONE

1. Milton Rokeach, *Beliefs, Attitudes, and Values: A Theory of Organization and Change* (San Francisco: Jossey-Bass, 1968), 16.
2. M. Scott Peck, *The Different Drum: Community Making and Peace* (New York: Touchstone, 1987).

CHAPTER 2: WHERE DO YOU STAND?

1. Charles H. Dodd, *Dynamics of Intercultural Communication* (New York: McGraw-Hill, 1998), 276.
2. "Jeremiah Wright Quotes," Search Quotes, http://www .searchquotes.com/quotation/In_the_21st_century,_white _America_got_a_wake-up_call_after_9+11+01._White _America_and_the_western_w/192179/.
3. James M. Kouzes and Barry Z. Posner, *Credibility: How Leaders Gain and Lose It, Why People Demand It* (San Francisco: Jossey-Bass, 1993), 14.
4. Jim Jones, "Crusade: Latino Catholics Boost Graham Crusade Attendance," *Christianity Today*, May 19, 1997, http://www .christianitytoday.com/ct/1997/may19/7t6051.html.
5. Jones.

CHAPTER 3: WHAT BRINGS PEOPLE TOGETHER?

1. Henry Abbott, "The Problem of Manu's Skin," *True Hoop*, June 25, 2005, http://espn.go.com/blog/truehoop/post/_/id/163/ the-problem-of-manu-s-skin.
2. James Ryle, "Grace—God's Unspeakable Gift," Identity Network, http://www.identitynetwork.org/apps/articles/default .asp?articleid=71830&columnid=.
3. David Jeremiah, *Captured by Grace: No One Is Beyond the Reach of a Loving God* (Nashville: Integrity, 2006), 11.
4. "Most Americans See Lingering Racism—in Others," CNN, December 12, 2006, http:// www.cnn.com/2006/US/12/12/ racism.poll/index.html.
5. "Most Americans See Lingering Racism—in Others."

CHAPTER 4: ARE YOU RACIALLY ATTRACTIVE?

1. Justo L. Gonzalez, *Out of Every Tribe and Nation: Christian Theology at the Ethnic Roundtable* (Nashville: Abingdon, 1992).
2. William B. Gudykunst and Young Yun Kim, *Communicating with Strangers: An Approach to Intercultural Communication* (New York: McGraw-Hill, 1997), 167.

CHAPTER 5: TEARING DOWN BARRIERS

1. Milton Rokeach, *Beliefs, Attitudes, and Values: A Theory of Organization and Change* (San Francisco: Jossey-Bass, 1968).
2. Larry A. Samovar and Richard E. Porter, *Intercultural Communication* (Belmont, CA: Wadsworth Publishing, 1982), 23.

3. Anne Lamott, *Bird by Bird: Some Instructions on Writing and Life* (New York: Anchor Books, 1995), 237.
4. Mother Teresa, "Teresa Tells the Truth," Harvard's Class Day Exercises, June 9, 1982, http://www.columbia.edu/cu/augustine/arch/teresa82.html.

CHAPTER 6: THE POWER OF FORGIVENESS

1. Leon Morris, *The Gospel According to John*, The New International Commentary on the New Testament (Grand Rapids, MI: Eerdmans, 1971), 617.
2. Oswald Chambers, *My Utmost for His Highest* (Uhrichsville, OH: Barbour Publishing, 2000), 250.
3. "Africa Calls for Slavery Apology," CNN.com/World, http://archives.cnn.com/2001/WORLD/africa/09/01/durban.slavery.
4. "Africa Calls for Slavery Apology."
5. Olga Idriss Davis, "Snoop, Dig, and Resurrect: What Can Scholars of African American Communication Learn from the Tulsa Race Riots of 1921?" *The Electronic Journal of Communication* 13, nos. 2 and 3 (2003), http://www.cios.org/EJCPUBLIC/013/2/01321.html.
6. "Forgiveness Quotes," Creating Positive Change, http://www.creating-positive-change.com/forgiveness-quotes.html.
7. Phil Hirschkorn, "Priest's Testimony Frees Man from Prison," CNN.com/LawCenter, July 24, 2001, http://archives.cnn.com/2001/LAW/07/24/priest.confession.ruling.
8. Stuart Wolpert, "Brain Reacts to Fairness as It Does to Money and Chocolate, Study Shows," UCLA Newsroom, April 21, 2008, http://newsroom.ucla.edu/portal/ucla/brain-reacts-to-fairness-as-it-49042.aspx?link_page_rss=49042.
9. "Emotional Megawati Apologizes to Aceh," CNN World, September 8, 2001, http://articles.cnn.com/2001-09-08/world/indon.aceh.visit_1_acehnese-aceh-province-apology?_s=PM:asiapcf.
10. Amit Baruah, "Megawati Apologises to Aceh, Irian Jaya," *The Hindu*, August 17, 2001, http://www.hinduonnet.com/2001/08/17/stories/0317000e.htm.
11. Stanley Hauerwas, *The Peaceable Kingdom: A Primer in Christian Ethics* (Notre Dame, IN: University of Notre Dame Press, 1991).

CHAPTER 7: TURNING THEORY INTO PRACTICE

1. Chris Chase, "Michael Phelps Eats 12,000 Calories Per Day," Yahoo Sports, August 13, 2008, http://sports.yahoo.com/blogs/olympics-fourth-place-medal/michael-phelps-eats-12-000-calories-per-day--olympics.html?.tsrc=rawlbs?date=20120510.
2. Edmund Jenks, "USS Intrepid Freed from Thick NYC Mud," Now Public Crowd Powered Media, December 5, 2006, http://www.nowpublic.com/uss_intrepid_freed_from_thick_nyc_mud.
3. Matthew S. Granovetter, "The Strength of Weak Ties," *American Journal of Sociology* 78, no. 6 (May 1973): 1360–1380.
4. Thomas Kochman, *Black and White Styles in Conflict* (Chicago: University of Chicago Press, 1981), 3.
5. Malcolm Gladwell, *Blink: The Power of Thinking Without Thinking* (New York: Little, Brown, 2005), 77.

CHAPTER 8: MODELING RECONCILIATION

1. Gordon W. Allport, *The Nature of Prejudice* (New York: Addison-Wesley, 1979), 14–15.
2. David Van Biema, "Can Megachurch Bridge the Racial Divide?" *Time Magazine*, January 11, 2010, http://www.time.com/time/magazine/article/0,9171,1950943,00.html.
3. James S. Hewett, *Illustrations Unlimited: Topical Collection of Hundreds of Stories, Quotations and Humor for Speakers, Writers, Pastors and Teachers* (Wheaton, IL: Tyndale, 1988), 249.
4. Viktor E. Frankl, *Man's Search for Meaning* (Boston: Beacon Press, 2006), 105.

CHAPTER 9: A PLACE TO STAND

1. William B. Gudykunst and Young Yun Kim, *Communicating with Strangers: An Approach to Intercultural Communication* (New York: McGraw-Hill, 1997), 17.
2. James Montgomery Boice, *Foundations of God's City: Christians in a Crumbling Culture* (Downers Grove, IL: InterVarsity, 1996), 22.

ABOUT THE AUTHOR

DAVID D. IRELAND, PhD, is founder and senior pastor of Christ Church, a multisite church in Montclair and Rockaway, New Jersey, with a six-thousand-member congregation of more than forty nationalities. Diversity consultant to the National Basketball Association, he leads chapel services for the New York Giants and New York Jets. He is the author of approximately twenty books and has appeared on *Dr. Phil*, *CBS Evening News*, and *The 700 Club*.

Ireland holds an undergraduate degree in mechanical engineering, a graduate degree in civil engineering, a master's degree in theology, and a doctorate degree in organizational leadership. He was recently appointed to the Governor's Advisory Commission on Faith-Based Initiatives. He also serves on the boards of Nyack College and Alliance Theological Seminary and was an adjunct professor at Drew University. He and his wife, Marlinda, have been married since 1984 and have two daughters, Danielle and Jessica.